PRAYERS AND MEDITATIONS
OF THE
QUERO APACHE

PRAYERS AND MEDITATIONS

OF THE

QUERO APACHE

MARIA YRACÉBÛRÛ

PHOTOGRAPHS BY LYNDA YRACÉBÛRÛ

Bear & Company
Rochester, Vermont

Bear & Company
One Park Street
Rochester, Vermont 05767
www.InnerTraditions.com

Bear & Company is a division of Inner Traditions International

Library of Congress Cataloging-in-Publication Data

Yracébûrû, Maria.
  Prayers and meditations of the Quero Apache / Maria Yracébûrû;
photographs by Lynda Yracébûrû.
    p. cm.
  ISBN 1-59143-024-0
  1. Prayers. 2. Meditations. 3. Spiritual life. 4. Apache Indians—
Religious life—Miscellanea. I. Title.

  BL560.Y73 2004
  299.7'825043—dc22

                                    2004041112

Printed and bound in Canada at Transcontinental Printing

10 9 8 7 6 5 4 3 2 1

Text design and layout by Priscilla Baker
This book was typeset in Goudy, with Papyrus and Gill Sans used as
display typefaces

Dedicated to the Quero Teñeh Chiricahua Chihinne Tlish Diyan, past and present.
This book goes out to the Directions with the blessings of the Ancient Ones.
I pray that each individual it reaches may see through the eyes of heart and feel the soft touch of Spirit, for as the soul quickens and embraces the higher, deeper, nobler, and greater things of life, so too do individuals live a life of empowerment as responsible co-creators of our reality.

Contents

Acknowledgments

For the opportunity to present these words given by courtesy of the Ancestors, with constant guidance generously provided, I wish to thank Nakía and Kato'ya, Tlish Diyan guardians; Phillip Cassadore, Paul and Jewel Yracébûrû, Ten Bears, and Naylin Lagé; Nochaydelklinne (the Dreamer) of the Apache; Tantoo Cardinal, Mathew King, and Frank Fools Crow of the Lakota; Buffalo Jim of the Seminole; Rita Coolidge and J. T. Garrett of the Cherokee; Rolling Thunder of the Cherokee/Shoshone; Kachada of the Hopi; Small Oak and Joanne Dove of the Connecticut; Keili'i Reichel of the Hawaiian Kahuna lineage; Don Jose of the Huichol; Billy Yellow of the Navajo; Grandpa, Grandma, and Perhan of Romani; John Heard; Nick Mancuso; Wayne Price of the Klingit; Storyteller of the Wampanoag; Marcellas Bearheart of the Muskogee/Creek; Mor Thiam of the Digon from Sengal, Africa; and my granddaughters, Marianna and Gabriella.

I am especially grateful to N. Scott Momaday, whose simple letter of support in 1971 convinced me to stay in school and write. My thanks are due also to Dr. Sharron Stroud, Gregg Braden, Dr. Alberto Villoldo, Brooke Medicine Eagle, Kalei Muller, Woody Bailey, Kilipaka Ontai, Arielle Ford, Dr. Gwendalle Cooper, Stephanie Gunning, Lee Awbrey, Katherine Suzuki, Kevin

Thomas, Adrienne Bench, Scott Smith, Jack Ore, Laurie Seaman, Alora Sudán, Franklin Damron, Anankha Chandler, and Jini, Connie, Peter, and Charlie. I would like to express my appreciation particularly to our sons Jeremy and Jason Tucker, who have given my life purpose and our tradition meaning.

And to my housthé, Lynda Yracébûrû, who gave encouragement, shared the journey, and nurtured me along the way.

Foreword

The prophecies of the Native Americas speak of a time that the world is entering now, a time of great cleansing and purification. The Hopi call this the time of Koyanasquatsi, of life out of balance. During this era humanity will be absorbed by materialism, will place greater value in the ways of the world than in the ways of Spirit. Brother will turn against brother, the once pristine rivers will be polluted with chemical waste, and the air will become unbreatheable. Then a great upheaval and awakening will occur. The Inca speak about this as the Pachacutti, when the world will be turned upside down. We are at this time right now.

The Pachacutti refers to the end of time and the dawning of a new era. All religions in the world forecast the end of time. In Christianity this event will be accompanied by a final judgment, when the deserving will recover their original, undying nature. In Judaism, the Messiah will come at the end of time. In the Christian cosmology, the old time ended with the coming of Christ and a new era began, which today we refer to as the Common Era, or C.E.

In the Native Americas, the dawning of the new era is predicted by many to begin in the year 2012, the starting date of the calendar of the Maya. In the Americas there is no

Messiah figure who will come to make the world right. Instead, the task will fall to each one of us as we discover ways to live in peace and balance with Earth. In the process, a new kind of human will appear on Earth. In fact, the Mayan calendar suggests that humanity has not yet appeared on Earth; the Mayan cosmology offers that we are protohumans, that the first truly human beings will appear in a decade.

Seers and prophets have predicted the signs foretelling this change. Among the Inca the old people speak of the time when the eagle of the north will fly with the condor of the south. They speak about the wrath of our father, the Sun, made manifest by the opening of the ozone hole over South America. All of these signs have come to pass. What remains now is for us to have the courage to evolve into a new human that can bypass the impulses for fear, aggression, and predatory behavior programmed into our prehuman brains.

The wisdomkeepers of the Americas developed spiritual processes for bypassing and regulating the destructive instincts in humans. These spiritual technologies transformed fear into love, scarcity into plenty, aggression into cooperation. These spiritual teachings allow us to participate consciously in our future evolution. They all begin with the practice of silence and stillness. They all awaken the reservoir of light energy that we carry within us, which can fuel our journey to our becoming.

These are the teachings and practices that Maria Yracébûrû shares with us with elegance and power. It is the knowledge she learned from Grandfather Ten Bears, which she has distilled into a fine elixir through a wisdom born of years of being tempered by lightning and wind. As you turn the pages of this book you will feel as if the wind itself is teaching you with her soft song. It is a song that I myself have heard many times in the breeze, for I was privileged to study and learn with the Q'ero elders of Peru, distant cousins of the

Quero Apache. They share a similar body of teaching of the luminous nature of the world, and the ways that we can be of service to each other, to nature, and to all of creation.

Take a deep breath. Know that this is the same breath that blew through the Amazon, the same breath that Ten Bears, the Buddha, and the Christ breathed. Listen to this wind.

ALBERTO VILLOLDO, PH.D.
AUTHOR OF *SHAMAN, HEALER, SAGE*

talking softly of stars
we lie upon velvet grass
gazing up, traveling.
truth pulses in my throat—
galaxies making me smile,
sensations of floating—
light calls through shimmering veils.
later, wakening
from dreams of Kato'ya's schemes.
flutter to Changing Mother
ten thousand years ago,
i move through moments.
in the night,
my back presses the magic
earth,
with my housthé.
we are love itself.

bízhí bikashe tú

Writing on the Water

Yo'ii t'aazhi' shíí daashizhoo ukehé,
Looking behind I am filled with gratitude.
Yo'ii bidááh shíí daashizhoo bil'onaagodah,
Looking forward I am filled with vision.
Yo'ii-áá shíí daashizhoo nalwod,
Looking upward I am filled with strength.
Yo'ii-o shíí daashizhoo gozhoo,
Looking within I discover peace.
Daaiina, And so it is.

Writing this book is an aspect and outcome of my training and is therefore part of the exciting and adventurous journey that I have come to know as life. The time spent writing this book has been a period of personal growth. As the Quero Apache say of such things, it has been a time of "potential and actualization."

I was given no intellectual description concerning Tutuskya, the Great Wheel of Life, as I was growing up, which caused me to comprehend the interplay of events with an understanding born of cellular knowing. This way of learning proved to be of great value in the circumstances that would play out as my life.

I write this book because I have come to realize how much of humanity's struggle and confusion can be transmuted with the simple practices I grew up with. As I was blessed to have sources of reference and traditional knowledge within my immediate environment, I was faced with some soul-searching and some important decisions to make. There were, no doubt, lessons for me in the sharing of my heritage. History has documented the efforts to quash Native culture and beliefs. Today very few individuals are left who carry the "original memory of evolution." The changing character of humanity has brought about periods of genocide, assimilation, programming, and rigid observance, the result being very wounded survival skills within Native America.

I grappled with this lineage history. Most notably, I was asking myself if it was appropriate to share these practices. However, the truth of evolution, of exploring greater potential, prevailed. I have watched all peoples open to their deeper and wiser selves. We are becoming who we always knew we could be. This is prophecy fulfilled. Humans evolve.

I want to put something across that is very powerful. Everything I do is born from the tradition I was taught by my grandfather, and the lessons of life I teach project from that tradition's spiritual life philosophy. I take the risk. I place my faith in prophecy and the vision of human potential that Grandfather Ten Bears instilled in me.

My grandfather, Ten Bears, was born in Pagotzinkay, Mexico, sometime between 1867 and 1870; he died at Bourke Canyon, Arizona, in 1973. Ten Bears came into contact at an early age with the Tlish Diyan philosophy and its heritage through his mother, Naylin Lagé, a Tlish Diyan healer and mystic who had apprenticed to her uncle, the Coyotero Apache dreamer and prophet Nochaydelklinne, the visionary responsible for the Salt River prophecies.* After growing up in Mexico in a renegade village of Apache, Ten Bears returned to the White Mountains of Arizona. His work, with its distinctions between natural and celestial magic, was in itself a call for relief of human suffering as a means of contributing to the spiritual evolution of humanity and the planet.

In this book I have tried to present, in a most understandable manner, the knowledge of connection inherent in the

---

*This stately medicine man's influence led to numerous gatherings in the late 1800s. The prophecies and teachings of evolution presented by Nochaydelklinne were considered hidden truths, to remain in sacred trust until the signs of nature revealed the designated time of sharing. Nochaydelklinne was assassinated in 1881.

teachings of my upbringing. I realize that not all will comprehend the message I and members of other indigenous communities worldwide present now, but I have faith that the power of these words will echo an understanding of inner knowing to quickening hearts everywhere.

There were once people who lived profoundly on this planet, people who lived in reciprocal, respectful relationship within the ecosystems of which they recognized themselves a part and whose sacred nature they knew and understood. These people lived lives in which their everyday actions were akin to, and in harmony with, the greater movements of the universe—they blended the sacred and the irreverent, the past and future, time and timelessness in the present moment. They were people who inherited an uninterrupted transmission of the knowledge of a way of being that stretched back to their mystical and distant ancestors. They knew the anatomy of the land in which they lived—they dreamed its dreams, learned what it taught, and felt the same pulse of life flowing through the veins of the universe that they heard singing within their own bodies. Some carry on this life philosophy today.

It is the lives and beliefs of such people, who held dynamic and vivid ways of experiencing and understanding the universe, ways that were far more precious, far truer and beyond anything modern scientific systems or interpretations of religion have been able to teach, that I honor here.

The time has come for humans to claim our true nature. We are joining, feeling the community of heart. Love, spiritual growth, and higher purpose magnify tenfold the ability of each of us to create these attributes in our own lives, and to assist others as they reach out. But to understand and walk paths of innate wisdom and insight we must acknowledge intuition and raise it to the centerpoint of human consciousness. We must claim our rightful inheritance of self, acknowledging our own insights and those of the wise ones, the elders, the guardians of knowledge of the Path of Beauty.

Humanity is now relearning and assimilating into daily life what has survived of the ancient knowledge to heal self, each other, and the planet. We are learning to pay homage and respect to others. Now we are hearing the voices of people who retained, or rediscovered, this ancient knowledge. We are learning and remembering through these teachers who, though many of them have roots that are nourished by souls of various cultures, are essentially the collective voice of one world spirit. The teachings from these wise ones, and our own dreams, analeptic memories, experiences, and changing awarenesses, are opening us up to what we had "forgotten." They are bringing us into transition. This transition is the realization of a need to re-turn, to turn in the circle, to rejoin the dance of life once more, to turn to the living paths that lead in the direction of our common home.

Two thousand years ago the ancestors of the Apache roamed as far north as Kansas, as far east as the Mississippi, as far south as Central America, and as far west as the Pacific Ocean. The Quero are understood to be "energy weavers," responsible for originating the traditions still practiced by the Quero Apache Tlish Diyan (Snake Clan).* I come to you this day to share with you what I have experienced as Tlish Diyan spirituality: a living-life belief system founded in the natural patterns of Earth and in universal energy flow, a way of living and being that bears witness to, perpetuates, and is a reminder of what the Ancient Ones called our "true identities."

The prayers and meditations you will find contained within these pages are filled with the beautiful poetic vision of my ancestors. The tradition of the Quero Apache, the energy weavers, teaches a profound practice of quieting the mind to come into energetic communication with All Our Relations. By moving through the spirals of this basic and impeccable practice we gather the tools of love: we embody esteem, confidence, respect,

---

*Tlish Diyan has interchangeable translations: Snake Clan, Snake Medicine, Snake Energy.

understanding, acceptance, and forgiveness of self and others. In this book I express these teachings in the language I learned from the forest and the desert, the landscape of my family's knowing. It is a way of expression borne of direct experience, and by being involved with one's whole being in constant interaction with Tutuskya, the Great Wheel of Life.

The arrowhead necklaces worn by my family are a Tlish Diyan reminder of the protection that truth and integrity allow for. My family's dedication to the practical application of Tlish Diyan teachings means that we believe in tolerance as a guiding principle of all spiritual philosophies, especially in a core issue such as defining the objective of a spiritual search. We define spirituality as the ability to embrace potential while understanding limitations, and to walk life's path with hope and integrity.

My family's dedication to the spiritual path for all beings is the reason I have written this book. I have likely not said anything here that has not been said many times before. And although this book was written with great love for All My Relations, it is truly the fulfillment of one ancient Apache's dream. Teaching in this manner is most untraditional in Quero lifeways, but it is recognized that the need has arisen to reach as many people as are open to the information at this time.

Prayers and Meditations of the Quero Apache describes my experiences with Grandfather Ten Bears. Through the philosophical insights and practice instructions I hope you receive some feeling of the atmosphere of inner peace that can be known, and confidence that can be gained, by walking this remarkable Wheel of Life.

This book, however, is not only a manual of shamanic practice. I ask you to experience the silence between heartbeats. Listen to your soul . . . allow yourself just to be.

May peace and love flow over you as you take the first step into the silence and follow the ancestors' tracks. Good journey, my friend.

IN THE BEGINNING

doohwaa-gon'ch'aada

Entering
the Silence

Evolution means becoming . . .

I was born a dreamer. I could hear things, see things, understand things without encountering them on the physical plane. Animals would talk to me and I would know what action to take. In my dreams I would learn about certain individuals and ways to assist them. In the dreamtime I could communicate with those from long ago.

Although I was born with many abilities, they were sharpened through walking the Path of Beauty and embracing Tutuskya, the Great Wheel of Life. Because of the teachings of Tutuskya, I can be empty. When you are "empty" Spirit can express itself as wisdom; it can heal the body with our own medicine power—our energetic perspective of life—and help us resonate with the universe as an integral part of All That Is.

Entering the Silence—cultivating personal times of no thought—is the practice at the heart of the Tlish Diyan life philosophy. By performing this daily ritual we release what we don't need—what no longer resonates to the energy of love—and replace it with the unconditional nurturance that we can receive from the universe. It is often during my practice of Entering the Silence that I receive the ceremonies, prayers, healing insights, and lessons that I share with you in this book.

Entering the Silence was a vital part of life in Grandfather Ten Bears' house; as a philosophy and a practice it held priority over all things. Our time in silence was serious endeavor for us. We'd go out into the canyon when the weather would allow so that we might be closer to the energies of the sacred Mother and be blessed by the warmth of Grandfather Sun's healing rays. We would address the Directions and our personal guides.

Then, according to the lunar progression, we would address the totems (animal and plant allies) that represented the energy of that part of the Changing Mother's cycles. I would watch, listen, and support Grandfather in his time, until he signaled that he was finished. It was my duty to bear witness to the gift of his prayers to the world, so that they might manifest in our combined reality. Then it would be my turn, and Grandfather would honor me by being my guardian.

I remember first participating in this type of ritual when I was about six or seven years old. Grandfather had taken me to the very top of the Spirit Cliffs at twilight that evening. The trail twisted and turned as we climbed, with rocks rising up like towering walls. Below we could see the cottonwoods and peach trees that cooled our canyon home. Up the canyon walls the setting sun unfolded in gold and copper play, stopping at the dark band of azure blue we saw as we reached the top. There was magic about us. The wind whipped around us and I was afraid of the heights at first. But as I said my prayers and connected to the various directional energies, a calmness came over my being and the winds faded. When I was done Grandfather gave me the warmest smile that I had ever seen cross his face.

I think this moment was crucial in my learning the Tlish Diyan philosophies. It occurred to me that this was the second sign that confirmed the prophecies Grandfather Ten Bears had received of my life (the first sign being my birth as it had been foretold four generations prior by Nochaydelklinne).

My medicine power was very strong on that day at the Spirit Cliffs, and from that point on Grandfather Ten Bears and I became nearly inseparable. Grandfather began to advise me about the ways of Spirit and humans alike and about how I should approach my destiny. He taught me the importance of emptying my mind when I would enter the silence and of generally developing a strong belief in my connection to All That Is. Without any of idea of how I knew this, I began to understand what Grandfather meant when he said that I was Tlish Diyan, and that I would take these practices into a period of new understanding. You see, Tlish Diyan teachings are a living-life philosophy—ever evolving and ever-changing with the energies of human perception and co-creation. This is the way all humans must be—ever evolving, ever changing—to reach the truth of who we are and what our purpose in being here is.

Grandfather Ten Bears' spirit was such that he refused to be disturbed by anything during his time of silence. When a person was gravely ill and seeking Grandfather's counsel, Grandfather instructed me not to disturb him if he was in prayer, for it was in this fashion that Grandfather would receive what he would need to be in service to the higher power of that person. Grandfather taught me that it was during this time of conscious connection to All That Is that the person's higher spirit would intertwine with Grandfather's and give Grandfather the symbology and direction necessary to assist in a healing or a crossover (death ritual). From Grandfather Ten Bears I learned that connection, energetic relationship, was the key to all solutions.

From childhood my life revolved around my studies of the traditional ways. I practiced entering the silence three times a day. When I was sitting in silence, I could feel all that was negative within me flowing out and something energetic and alive flowing in. I felt like I was sitting in the middle of one huge flame, being kissed by the fire of transmutation but never burned.

Years later, after straying from this path, I became very ill. Suddenly I knew that the only way to heal myself was to return to the ways of my ancestors. Following three days of an extreme fever, I prayed for a sign that I was to follow the tracks of the ancestors, living and teaching a traditional lifestyle in these contemporary times, and that I was to be with my housthé (lifemate), Lynda. I asked that the sign be so blatant that even I couldn't miss it. Lynda and I were living in the Bay Area at the time. It snowed that morning, and because it never snows in San Francisco I took this to be the unmistakable sign I requested.

This period of reestablishing my connection was to prove critical for my future, both in helping me to learn about myself and to embrace the community I now work through. Although for a while after my return I found entering the silence to be quite difficult and I felt no apparent energy shifts, with persistence I finally began to feel faint stirrings. And though this movement seemed to take place only inside my body, by praying to my guardian, Nakía, for strength, I was able to cultivate that tiny, unseen stirring until it flowed out through my body as the rocking movement of the Tlish Diyan snake dance.

I began a daily practice of entering the silence. Two or three times a day I walked in the orchard where we lived, feeling beneath me the energy of the Great Mother. It was such a peaceful place to heal. I felt as though I was absorbing all the good energy of the universe. I felt that I had returned home.

This was an important time in which I embraced my family of Spirit. I began a period of deep learning about the cyclic ceremonies we call *diyi'ni hedowachee* (holyway festivals of joy) and how they work in relationship to aligning the magnetics of the planet with those of humanity. My education demonstrated with great certainty how we are all interconnected. I learned how certain energies relate to certain types of healing. When I recognized that a place carried depressed energy it appealed to me to hold life-affirming celebrations to raise the *ihi'-dahí* (life force), and I could feel the ceremony working. Joining together in circle, those of us gathered would concentrate on the planet until it became as though we were looking through a glass and could see all of life upon Earth functioning in harmony. At these times I became totally focused; it was as if all present were in another realm. At many of our festivals we would dance to raise the energetic vibration and achieve maximum potential for healing; our dance movements wouldn't stop until we could feel the heat rising from the flame of transmutation.

These ceremonies were easily one day long; many times such ceremonies would last two or three days. By entering the silence and asking the question, "How can I assist in the healing of Changing Mother and of humanity's soul?" I was given answers.

After my hiatus, in coming back to the practice of Entering the Silence I understood the reasons I lived the difficult life I had experienced—how everything that had happened to me in the past and the refocusing of the present was all in preparation for my future. My education demonstrated with great certainty how all in the universe is interconnected.

TLISH DIYAN PHILOSOPHY

In the Tlish Diyan philosophy the cosmos is an interacting and reciprocating energetic process. It is a totally inclusive energy field—a universe in which an observer cannot be considered as separate from what is under observation but instead is an essential part of it.

The Tlish Diyan description of the universe is that of an "ocean" of primordial energy that is both unmanifested and unconditioned but, at the same time, is given to manifesting in a multitude of ways and at various vibratory frequencies. That which is unmanifested is imbued with and animated by this same energy; in other words, there is no fundamental difference between this primordial energy in its abstract, unconditioned state and in its manifested forms. The manifested and conditioned and the unmanifested and unconditioned are both aspects of one reality.

To extend the analogy of the ocean, it is as though in manifest form the water has frozen into lumps to become matter. Eventually these lumps melt back into the main body of the ocean while freezing takes place in other areas, producing different "denser" or "solid" pieces of ocean. This process of freezing, melting, and refreezing is continuous and infinite, constantly repeating itself over eternity.

The universe is a harmonious whole, a continuum in which every "thing" resonates with, reflects, and is reflected by every other "thing." That is to say, in this universe no one element of existence can fundamentally be considered to be isolated from any other element, nor indeed can one "thing" be truly described without describing every other "thing." While in ordinary states of consciousness we experience a universe of diversity and difference, in heightened states of awareness all aspects of the universe are understood to share the same nature, to be one. We live in a universe in which everything is essentially both the same and different—two aspects of the same reality.

We are part of a living, energetic universe that is in a perpetual flow of change and evolution. In its raw state this energy is the life breath of all existence; it forms different dimensional realms, many of them invisible within our commonly accepted reality. Although most of us are usually unaware of these other "unseen" levels of existence, these realms nevertheless interpenetrate and reciprocate with this plane of reality. No separation exists; there are no separate realities, except in the inability to apprehend, identify, or know them.

But there have always existed people, in different cultures and at various times, who possess the ability to cross the invisible bridges to the unseen, and who know how to tap into and work with this life-giving energy in its supreme state. This energy has been known since the earliest times, when we traced its terrestrial arteries as a network of meridians, or ley lines, across the land. Our ancestors founded sacred centers at certain places along these lines where the energy flow was at its most powerful or most accessible to being worked with for spiritual, magical, or therapeutic purposes.

Tlish Diyan practices address and access this universal energy in relation to humanity, Earth, and evolution. To evolve beyond the linear thinking process into a truly multidimensional universal consciousness, a being connected to All That Is, we must first ask ourselves: "What is the goal of life?" Many people look for some grand meaning to life; the answer to the question about the goal of life still eludes thousands of years after the question was first posed. Many people are rather unhappy today because they have unrealistic expectations and desires of themselves, of the people around them, and of the world in general.

Evolution comes as a consequence of the natural human desire for guidance and understanding in the ways the world operates. The goal of Tlish Diyan teachings is simple: to help individuals live happier and healthier lives by connecting to all our potential, touching All Our Relations with our essence, and freeing our spirit from illusional fear. The Quero Apache Tlish Diyan firmly believe that as individuals claim the empowerment discovered in healing connection, we become fully present in the moment and consciously aware of our feelings of power. This contributes strength, stability, and healing from within us out into the world. We make responsible choices and co-create in affirmation of all life.

Tlish Diyan philosophy teaches us how to:

1. understand the principles of nature
2. understand the principles of and motivations behind community structure

3. understand the principles that govern and motivate us as individuals, and
4. understand the dynamic relationships between all that exists.

By gaining a clear comprehension of the principles of nature and the interrelationships between nature, humanity, and the individual, we can then possess a clear picture of the world and our place within it. With this understanding we have the tools with which to eliminate much personal confusion, and thus encourage personal empowerment. The absurdity and chaos of life diminish when we access the energetic flows within the self and the universe. The Tlish Diyan teachings give us the tools to understand what must necessarily be attended to for humans to live happier lives.

The teachings of Grandfather Ten Bears describe sixty-two different forms of energy in the universe. This energy is named Guzhuguja juulgu, which literally translates as "proper balance and harmony encircled." The teachings describe *ihi'dahí*, "life force," as having two complementary aspects: Yusn, the "Giver of All Life," corresponding to all attributes associated with the masculine energies in nature; and Esonkñhsendehé, "Changing Mother the Earth," relating to all that is female-creative energy. Humanity receives the masculine aspect from above, from the universe or sky, while it receives the feminine aspect from below, from the earth. These two energetic aspects are known to the Quero as the Sacred Parents.

The directional flow of these energies in the human body is depicted by two entwined snakes following the poles along the spine. These two complementary aspects of Guzhuguja juulgu come together in the human body at a point in the lower belly, roughly two inches below the navel and deep in the body's interior—a point called *bibiiye'* (all energy together). It is here, at the energetic and gravitational center of the body, that this energy can be transmuted into spiritual energy, literally creating physical heat. Raising this energy in the human body in such a way that it flows through a subtle system of nerves up the spinal column has the effect of opening energy centers on its path, balancing human magnetics with the planetary magnetic flows, and finally arousing innate wisdom or cosmic consciousness.

One of the ways in which a person's life energy interacts with the environment is electromagnetically. It is a simple matter to demonstrate that the body emits an electrostatic field; there are substantial differences in the readings of those people who are full of vitality in comparison with those who are in poor health. The planet Earth also emits its own energy field in which our personal energy fields breathe and "feed." Each and every moment each living person is transmitting signals through this terrestrial energy field at frequencies that most human beings are unaware of. People who have tapped the *ihi'-dahí*, the life force, in the body can, through interaction with the earth's electromagnetic field, extend their own field over vast distances in powerful, concentrated, coherent patterns. This is the basis for what is known as "manifesting vision."

In Tlish Diyan philosophy, humanity is understood as living in a shared cosmos that is mysterious and expresses profound spiritual evidence of the divine power behind all natural phenomena. All of nature is considered sacred, its beauty appreciated as a bridge between human consciousness and the sacred. According to Tlish Diyan teachings, the purpose of human life is to act on behalf of *ihi'dahí* through life-affirming ritual. It is the principles and practices of this energetic exchange that I was taught as Tlish Diyan.

THE QUERO GREAT WHEEL OF LIFE

Diyi is the spiritual energy of the universe, the energy from which the world was created. *Diyi* exists in all living things. Because *diyi* is of cosmic origin its source is elusive and mysterious, but its manifestations are real and can be accessed in Tlish Diyan practices. Individuals create a link to the source of *diyi*, or medicine power, by connecting with ancestors and spirit guides in rituals and ceremonies. These connections bring us closer to All That Is to help us clarify and commit to our path.

This spiritual connection makes us mentally stronger, less confused, and able to heal issues of the past with a clear understanding of the sacredness of life. The stronger the connection between us and All That Is, which is also All Our Relations, the clearer the picture of the world and our place within it.

Growth—the expansion of self-awareness for life-affirming purposes—is achieved through circular, spiraling motion, which the ancestors call *shi tsuye tlendil*, "four spiraling together," a term that evokes the power of the circle. The first three ascending spirals of Tutuskya—*nohwizá'yé biké'é* ("following the ancestors' tracks"), *nohwizá'yé zhiheego* ("living in the way of the ancestors"), and *nohwizá'yé bi kigoya'íí* ("sharing ancestral wisdom")—begin and are completed within this life experience. Though begun here, the fourth spiral—actually, the hub of the spiral—*nohwizá'yé bizhíí* ("speaking with the ancestor's voice"), is completed by few during this earthwalk. For most it is a spiral traveled through the transition of death and rebirth.

The magnetic directional energies of South, Southwest, West, Northwest, North, Northeast, East, and Southeast contained within this sacred spiral describe the conditions that characterize the state of human existence and the way to transcend that existence and are considered the core of Tlish Diyan power. On this Path of Beauty, the human condition is

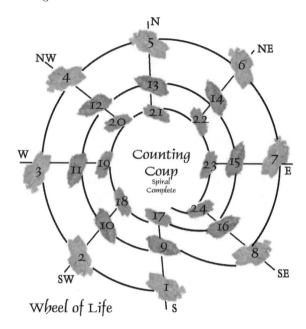

Wheel of Life

THE QUERO GREAT WHEEL OF LIFE

The Quero Great Wheel of Life is a map, charting aspects along our life journey. It can be used in three ways.

- Addressing the directional energies for guidance:
  South = Unity/healing disconnection
  Southwest = Nature/discovering spontaneity
  West = Ease/releasing tension
  Northwest = Flow/tapping energy
  North = Authentic power/inner direction
  Northeast = Harmony/inner and outer peace
  East = Nurturing/time and rest
  Southeast = Beauty/self-purpose

- Traveling the individual spirals to connect to community:
  Outer Spiral = Truth/discovering true self
  Middle Spiral = Change/implementing truth in life
  Inner Spiral = Peace/wisdom
  Hub = Actualization

- Walking the individual stones on the spiral to help us develop and grow and transform:
  1. Heron—Aggressive Healing: Beginning the path
  2. Coyote—Trickster: Energy and intent

3. Wolf—Teacher Within: Sacred laws
4. Bear—Introspective Healing: Transformation
5. Goose—Endurance in Our Quest: Initiation
6. Buffalo—Prayer and Abundance: Fear
7. Condor—Whirling Rainbow Dream: Releasing
8. Hummingbird—Joy: Simplicity
9. Flicker—Protection from Negativity: Finding center
10. Hawk—Vision Manifesting: Exploring duality
11. Deer—Gentleness: Creating joy
12. Puma—Leadership by Example: Harmony
13. Parrot—Healing through Unconditional Love: Natural cycles
14. Horse—Balanced Power: Finding answers
15. Owl—Seeing through Deception: Timing
16. Eagle—Spirit Within: Transcending chaos
17. Crow—Original Memory: Being a leader
18. Otter—Playfulness: Being at one
19. Roadrunner—Mental Agility: Unconditional love
20. Snake—Transmutation: Responsible co-creation
21. Frog—Cleansing: Resolving
22. Butterfly—Gentle Transformation: Cooperation
23. Turtle—Earth Connection: Community of heart
24. Bat—Rebirth: Birth a new world

described as one of disconnection due to basic illusions regarding the true nature of existence. These illusions about the nature of reality cause us to live lives centered around the idea of a permanent and separate individual self. Attitudes and perceptions are supported by, and in turn support, a dualistic, discriminating, conditioned and perpetually conditioning consciousness, leading to actions that result in nothing but negativity and delusion. It is due to the nature of repeated actions and conditioned habitual patterns of behavior arising from within this illusion that, during the Fourth World of Separation, humanity was trapped in a continuous cycle of birth and death governed by the laws of cause and effect.

In the Quero legends of evolution there are seven worlds, or energetic time/space paradigms, all cohabitated by humans. Each world paradigm represents a specific commitment in the evolutional process of the combined consciousness. The Fourth World of Separation represents the darkest part of this timeline of humanity's history. Having been completed in all due sacredness, we now rise into a finer frequency known traditionally as the Fifth World of Peace and Illumination.

This prophetic shift in human consciousness has been foretold by many spiritual philosophies and is now recognized for its interactive displays of transition. The world evolves, much as it did during the Industrial Revolution, but at a scale of 13^{20}, a vibration that far surpasses anything previously known.

In realizing this jumpstart into human potential, attributes of empowerment are actualized by many so that we may responsibly co-create a reality of peace and harmony. The information presented on how best to work in this form of harmonic cooperation with the spiritual essence of Changing Mother and her children was outlined in the creation legends of time.

The teachings of Tutuskya, the Great Wheel of Life, point to a way of self-actualization through alignment with the directional forces, a prescription for the final transcendence of dualistic consciousness through healing dysfunction, removing illusion, and actualizing true identity. These teachings help lay into the body the understanding that the true nature of existence is continual change and evolution. The realization and experience of the essential non-self nature and oneness with the universe extinguishes all dualistic, conditioned behavior and liberates humanity from fear's illusion of isolation. This realization promotes responsible co-creative acts of empowerment, heightened awareness, and a magical sense of connection to the totality of All That Is and All Our Relations, resulting in a deep feeling of security and inner peace.

The way to self-actualization is through love. All spiritual philosophies carry the same underlying foundation—the belief that love is the ultimate healing energy. This is the principle behind the belief of human evolution, but to put it into practice the meaning of love needs to be constantly rediscovered. The way to rediscover this meaning is through the application of the timeless Tlish Diyan precept of "remembrance of true identity."

This was the double task set upon us eons ago: The aim of the Tlish Diyan is to channel energy to any individual who asks for help, and, as the principles of Tlish Diyan repeat time and again, to support the individual, humanity, and the planet in coming into harmonious alignment. Since the basis for success in this operation is the elimination of any selfish intentions, each person must undergo a process of self-healing and development to embrace full remembrance of connection. The Tlish Diyan teachings stress that the most important premise in life is love and life-affirming celebration. It also asserts that miracles are manifestations of natural laws that humanity has not yet fully come to understand.

Grandfather Ten Bears stated that "healing within the vastness of natural energy forces is possible through the emission of magnetism by the human heart and body, by which one individual acts on other people and on the environment around him." All applied magic, which Ten Bears described as "a shift in perspective," takes place through unconditional love.

Entering the Silence, one of the Tlish Diyan's central practices, thus aims at generating magnetism through embracing the prayer wheel, which Ten Bears explained as being a subtle form of energy that, like matter itself, has multiple attributes.

The wheel can be viewed as a type of web. As Linda Seger writes in her book *Web Thinking* (Inner Ocean Publishing, 2002):

> The connections and interdependence of Web thinking
> are at the very center of science, mathematics, psychology,

religion and medicine. Futurists such as Alvin and Heidi Toffler and Hazel Henderson believe we are in a time of transition, moving from one model to another—a paradigm emphasizing decentralization and symbiotic relationship. Web thinking can be the future model for feminists who have critiqued the Line, but are still searching for a more equal and integrative model. It can be a model for theologians, who recognize that our metaphors for God need to change if we are going to create a more just society and a more expansive spirituality. It can be a model for our business and personal lives as we seek to make our work and relationships more creative, more productive, joyful and collaborative.

As web thinkers, we use the Line to give us direction, the Circle to create teamwork and community, the Spiral to help us develop and grow and transform, and the Web to reach out, establish relationships, and connect.

As we begin to shift consciousness we embrace the linear/directional give and take, the challenge and support-system energies that Changing Mother Earth provides in her magnetic compass: South, the power of transmutation, direction of trust, emotions, and the inner child represented by the Snake totem; Southwest, the nurturing of the Thunderbeings and place of visioning, represented by Coyote; West, the direction of introspection, dreams, and physical healing, attended to by the Bear totem; Northwest, place of the Winds of Change and Sacred Universal Laws, presided over by the Little People (fairies, elves, and menahunes); North, direction of abundance, wisdom, prayer, and gratitude as overseen by the Buffalo totem; Northeast, the direction of gentle transformation and the great Master Teachers known as kachiñas; East, direction of illumination, clarity of Spirit, the fire of creativity, the energy of beginning and ending as observed by the Eagle totem; Southeast, the direction of genetic memory, the Ancestors, and the healing of all family situations, presided over by Puma; Above, the male energy of the cosmos and our Warrior spirit; Below, the female energy of the cosmos, the Mother nurturer we all claim as physical children of the Earth; Within, the higher spirit of each of us; and, finally, Without, the eternal guiding light of the totality of All That Is, mass consciousness, and the unconditional love of the Creative Source.

NOW WE BEGIN

Working the principles of the Tlish Diyan does not bring about a sudden and miraculous transformation of our state of being. It is more like receiving a seed that, once planted, we must nurture by providing the conditions necessary for its growth and development. Once received, commitment to the practice of Entering the Silence is essential, as it takes time for healthy patterning to take root within our experience and our cellular memory. We have a lot of bad habits to change. By developing our connection to All That Is and bringing it to maturity we become our "true selves," growing to our full potential as children of the universe and co-creators of our reality, and at the same time extending the duration of our earthwalk this time around.

Essential for daily personal ceremony is *doohwaa-gon'ch-aada* (entering the silence), or creating a time for no thought. An important assistant to coming into this state is creating a sacred space. This is a place where respect is honored above all things. It is a place you create that is yours alone and in which you seek sanctuary from the daily hubbub of life. It is a place where you must be totally honest with yourself and Spirit as you come to seek guidance, to be nurtured, and to honor those who assist you.

You might create an altar that holds items that you feel especially drawn to, feeling empowered in their presence, or your sacred space may be as simple as a candle. If you choose to create a visual manifestation of the Medicine Wheel I would suggest gathering eight items that each represent an attribute of the directions of the compass: South, Southwest, West, Northwest, North, Northeast, East, and Southeast. Place these items in a circle in a sunwise direction. In the center place a candle, which will provide a focal point during your prayers and meditation.

This altar can be a permanent fixture or one that is placed out only when you desire to seek a state of prayer. This sacred space represents your spiritual essence, and even if you are unaware of it at the time of construction, the items signify the guides that assist you in these uniquely powerful directional energies.

For this practice you will need a comfortable place to sit, preferably on the floor. However, if you suffer from back problems, sitting in a chair is acceptable. Your goal is to be in the silence for approximately thirty minutes each day. Don't worry if at first this is difficult to achieve. It is a good habit that needs to be established, and the more it is practiced and the time involved is lengthened, the easier it becomes.

No one should disturb you during this time. Turn off the telephone and the answering machine. Try to allow yourself maximum privacy. It is important to know and remember that the intent you bring into ceremony determines the power of the outcome.

Smudge is an important factor in setting the tone for your practice. Native Americans often use sage, cedar, sweetgrass, and snakeroot to "smoke off" the body and the space. Many other plants are used for smudging, but these are my personal favorites and the ones I grew up using. You may also use various essential oils or incenses to achieve the same effect.

Once all the elements are in place on your altar you will
burn the smudge of your choice, smoking yourself and your
altar. Smudge-smoking involves brushing the smoke over all
the items that will serve within this ritual as focal points or
power tools, to purify them. Make sure to smudge-smoke your
body as well.

In this book are prayers and meditations relating to the four
sacred spirals comprising Tutuskya, the Great Wheel of Life.
Within the first three of these spirals there are eight prayer
wheels—*naadin di'i'i*—and a short essay that addresses the
theme of that particular spiral. As you progress along the wheel
you will discover how the energy shifts and turns. Familiarize
yourself with the sensations of the different directional energies.

Each wheel begins with a prayer that opens the circle,
alerting those of the spiritual plane to your intent. This is followed by the directional prayers. Once the directional energies
have been addressed aloud and honored, stating affirmation of
growth, higher self, and partnership in conscious and responsible co-creation, the meditation phase begins.*

Begin the meditation by breathing from the belly, concentrating your awareness at the point roughly two inches below
the navel. This is the body's gravitational center and the place
where the two complementary aspects of *ihi'dahí*, the life force,
come together in the human body. Focus your vision upon the
candle flame within the center of your altar. When sensations
and feelings arise in the body, breathe into the places where
those sensations and feelings are lodged, bringing your attention to that place in the body and maintaining awareness of
the quality of the sensation without judging it as "negative" or

---

*The power of the spoken word is the power of manifestation, which is why Don
Miguel and many teachers of indigenous backgrounds warn us to be "impeccable
with our spoken word."

"positive." When thoughts arise attention can be brought back immediately to the breathing and body awareness.

The conscious act of breathing is, for Native Americans and peoples of many other indigenous cultures, an act of blessing. Breathing in deeply, we partake of the essence of prayer. Breathing out slowly, deliberately, we affirm breath as the living essence of the surrounding universe. Entering the Silence enhances health, opens the doors of the mind to learning, clears the intellect for coming to co-creative solutions, balances energies and emotions, and carries you to the Source. The whole practice of Entering the Silence is really performed as prayer and meditation. Grandfather Ten Bears defined the difference between prayer and meditation this way: "Prayer is speaking to Spirit. Meditation is being quiet long enough to hear Spirit's reply."

After breathing in this manner for a while, focusing on movement of energy in the body and emptying the mind, place both hands on the chest. Exhale as you brush the hands down the torso and along the thighs to the knees, then make a wide circle to come up to the shoulders. (See the photographs on the facing page, clockwise from upper left to lower right.) Bring the hands down to the chest and repeat the cycle twelve times. This number represents each of the directional energies you addressed in your opening prayers. You are now open to take the vibrational frequencies of Earth's magnetic directional support system in through your *ihi'dahí*. Pause for a moment and feel the intuitions of superconsciousness as they become permanent landmarks in your sacred identity, sources of continuing guidance, iridescent steps on a living, growing web of actualization.

Next, press the inner corner of each eyeball with the middle or second finger of each hand. (See the photograph at the lower left on page 27.) This alerts the autonomic nervous

system through the optic nerve and the motor nerve, and the nervous system responds with movements that are in harmony with the condition of your body at this time. The most common of these autonomic movements is a rocking motion. Let whatever movements arise be expressed through your body, directing energy to those parts that are blocked, tired, and in need of nurturing and healing.

When we are tired we are more inclined to immediately sabotage any efforts we may begin. We immediately align with our thoughts. This then is our first lesson: when we approach our ritual we must be clear in our level of intent. Our thoughts can be for higher vibrational sources of energy, harmony, and knowledge. These thoughts nurture us with glandular stimulation and so direct our whole organism. There occurs an interchange between limitless and varied forms of energy and the energies of life and of individual existence. The question at hand when you begin a session is will you be able to hold your energetic intent? If frustration enters, do something else that releases the pent-up energy and helps you relax. This frustration is an overamplifying of body and mind, which blocks Spirit. Leave and have some fun, then come back to your practice.

When beginning this practice some people may experience no spontaneous movement for a period of several months; for others, a rocking movement of the torso may begin in a circular movement to the right (in the Northern hemisphere) or to the left (in the Southern hemisphere). The movements will stop on their own, if allowed to come to completion. (However, many people will not allow themselves freedom in regard to time, so they stop the rocking movements prematurely.)

These spontaneous movements are followed by a period of deep meditational work, in which you focus any visions that creep across the tapestry of your mind into the candle flame.

This meditation time should be continued through its natural completion, but for a minimum of thirty minutes. The power of this experience will obviously vary according to your dedication to your growth, and therefore will be different from day to day, as will the visions received. Sometimes the energy shifts experienced in this practice may affect you for only that instant, or they may last a lifetime, depending on your willingness to address fears and walk through illusions created by the ego in an effort to block change.

Upon completion of the meditational phase of Entering the Silence devote a few moments to journalling about the experience. Keeping track of your experiences in this way reinforces the reality of the experience and charts milestones along the path for future introspective work.

As you progress with this daily personal ceremony, so too does your bodily and spiritual awareness. You develop a growing sensitivity to the energy flows and to the needs of different areas and this means that you can actively work on these areas (involving yourself or those you pray for) with your prayers during times of silence. This is really an extra-sensitive extension of the natural and unconscious manner in which we affect the surrounding waves of energy with our conscious, responsible thought patterns. I refer to this listening as the "call" of the soul; I have long been able to hear the "call" from individuals and the creatures of nature alike.

Often when we begin to pay attention to the voices within in this way we begin to experience our first real perception of the vibrational shift that can occur within our beings. We may have experienced this vibrational movement periodically in the past but were unconscious of the conditions precipitating it. The reason we have been unconscious of this process is due to imbalances within the body that have gone unnoticed in our normal day-to-day (distracted) state of attention. Our growing awareness of interdependence deepens our understanding of how the body, mind, and spirit are affected by emotional, physical, and spiritual experiences and environmental energies from day to day and, indeed, often during the course of just an hour.

The quality and feeling-tone of spontaneous fluxes while embracing the spirals of Tutuskya are quite different from the spontaneous shifts that result from the sudden release of energy that has been blocked within the body's musculature. The experiences felt during engagement with the Tutuskya prayer wheel are accompanied by a strong, positive, concentrated sensation, in contrast to the scattered, agitated quality that often accompanies the release of hitherto blocked energy in the body. This kind of release can occur throughout the transmutational practice of Entering the Silence. Bodywork can help ground these releases.

Spend a full lunar cycle working with each prayer wheel. Beginning on a new moon, enter the silence with a single prayer wheel (such as Heron) every day until the full moon, when you shift to the next prayer wheel (Coyote), and so on.

Walking the Path of Beauty and working the prayer wheel involve rites of passage. Celebrating these passages concentrates a great deal of energy in the body and then discharges it throughout the entirety of the cosmic web. So honor the completion of each spiral in a significant and life-affirming manner. Do something nice for yourself, and enjoy the camaraderie of friends; our support group—our friends—is the first manifestation of web consciousness. This brings a sensation of heat like a subtle fire, often accompanied by a buzzing or tingling electrical sensation up the back and along the arms and into the fingertips. This sensation is confirmation of your energetic connection being completely open and engaged in the vital interplay of life.

PRAYER: THE KEY TO MANIFESTING VISION

Prayer is important. Vocalizing words creates ripples in the cosmic web of life. Those who pray with their hearts and their souls discover unity with the essence of All That Is and make themselves clean conduits for manifestation, emerging, because of prayer, stronger and more empowered as responsible co-creators of our reality. The act of prayer, the revealing of oneself, the opening of the heart, binds us all together in unity.

Prayer equips us for life. Prayer is the means by which we attune ourselves to the higher forces. I do not mean prayer without realization, but praying with the soul and the mind, with an earnest desire to reach out to the highest the soul can attain. Then, filled with the inspiration that comes as a result of the prayer, we manifest responsibly that which is needed by All Our Relations.

Prayer is never wasted, for thought has potency. Thought also has universal application. By praying we release psychic energy, and this is used by our spiritual guides to partner with us in the co-creative acts of life.

When we pray with sincerity we make ourselves receptive to higher forces. The mere act of prayer opens up the soul. We pray with our hearts, souls, and minds. As we visualize the desired outcome while we pray—to such extent as to be able to taste, smell, feel, and love that outcome—in such a manner that we feel the desired outcome is already fulfilled, we manifest. Prayer, truly understood, is a great spiritual experience.

I can best explain this by saying that prayer is always to be regarded as a responsible act of life affirmation. There is no greater work, no greater love, no greater religion, no greater philosophy than to speak the words, "I pray on behalf of the children of the Directions and All My Relations."

The more we learn how to enter into sacred partnership—with our spirit guides and with All Our Relations—the more we help to ease the evolution of our world and develop the connection of Spirit within each of us. It is all very simple, and it matters not what traditional spirituality or religion you may originate within. All life-affirming ceremony moves us ever forward toward our combined destiny.

In everyone there is a search going on for that which is human divinity. When the part of us that is sacred is discovered, then we feel at one. We are being guided on paths that benefit all. Every day and every night there comes to us a band of spirit guides. Each one of them has come to assist us in manifesting conditions that produce a circle of life, with its illumination radiating to all areas of pain and suffering.

I ask you to remember that everyone, aware or unaware, is helping the plan of evolution, that great and wondrous design in which each of us is helping to weave our own little medicine blanket. The ways for healing humanity's soul are being revealed now, and every race and every color is shown to have its part in that healing. This is the emergence of the Fifth World of Peace.

What takes place when we enter the silence is but a part of the tapestry that is being woven. Day after day and night after night the work goes on, everyone helping to weave a mighty work of beauty that will one day comfort and nurture all within the web of life.

When prayer comes from the soul, when it is a prayer of pure intent and inspiration, a prayer that desires to reach out and create an envelope of love for self and All Our Relations, then the very desire with which it is being spoken gives it wings that will carry it to the heights of the realms of Spirit.

Prayer of this nature carries with it a power. How far that power can be transmuted into manifestation depends on faith. Do your words touch your heart with tearful joy? This is power.

Prayer that is prayer, that is inspiration, that is a desire for healing, for knowledge, for light, for wisdom, for guidance—all this is prayer that produces evolutional growth. Our mind is not only part of the body but also part of our spirit, and it has powers that come from Spirit. We are learning to use these powers through our evolution. This is what is being revealed to us at this time.

Prayer is the expression of the soul. Let me make that clear. It is the yearning of the soul that calls out for light, for guidance. That very act, of itself, brings an answer, because it is setting into motion the power of thought.

It is the cause that attracts a reply, which is the effect. There are spirit guides listening for our prayers, and when we pray we immediately attract all those on a spiritual plane with whom our prayers resonate. Prayer is the cause that attracts the effect of their reply. Because they desire to co-create with us, the power of these spirit guides adds to the power that we put forth on the ethers. In praying, we set into motion waves of thought that are part of Spirit. This enables the forces of the universe to partner with us in accordance with the Sacred Laws of evolution. By praying we make ourselves receptive to those forces with which we can make a difference.

Our Sacred Parents within, the spiritual aspects of All That Is, are perfect, and they seek to express themselves. As we allow this expression through prayer and through service, we are allowing the power of love that is within us to manifest vision. Prayer, service—whatever we seek to do that uplifts eases the path of evolution.

Prayer is the desire to express love, and that act enables the soul to manifest vision and to reach out to planes that before it could not reach. Through prayer we equip ourselves so that we can embrace more of life and thus receive more of the bounty of love to be found in life. The bountiful love of our

Sacred Parents for us is infinite, and our souls are infinite as we learn to express that infinity.

In our home are my sacred tools, my family artifacts, and altars honoring our connection to All Our Relations. Outside our home is a Medicine Wheel constructed of very beautiful, ancient stone people, traditionally aligning the landscape and those who visit. This Medicine Wheel is attended to with offerings of pollen, tobacco, water, sage, cedar, and sweetgrass. This Medicine Wheel brings miracles, and in turn we are reborn of one heart.

Now, as I work through my storytelling, traditional healing, and ceremonial facilitation, the Wheel endorses what I learned during my time with Grandfather Ten Bears and all that is to be known in the practice of Entering the Silence.

Become comfortable and begin your prayer wheel session. May your journey be all that you desire and more.

Ni'gosdzan 'awolzaana,
I come from the Earth Mother
Yaa' 'awolzaana,
I come from the Sky Father
Da'iltsé dagoyaana ni'gosdzan 'ildiizhé,
I come into this Circle to be all that I can be.
Pinu'u,
I am I
Shíí shi okahí,
This is my Prayer.
Daaiina.
And so it is . . .

nohwizá'yé bíké'é

Following the Ancestors' Tracks

As teachings grow in the world, it means the end of all separateness between peoples. It means the end of barriers. It means the end of racial distinctions, class distinctions, color distinctions, and distinctions between religious philosophies, for gradually we learn that we all carry an aspect of Spirit's truth inside, and that the part enshrined in the heart of each of us in no way contradicts that portion that is precious to others.

So out of the apparent confusion the pattern takes its shape, and harmony and peace come. I tell you these things so that we can understand the part that we who chose to manifest in this lifetime play in spiritual evolution, and the part that each one of us must play in that evolvement as history runs its course.

What I say fits with all the noble and elevated ideas that have come to the vision of all the seers, dreamers, and prophets who have attempted in every age to render service. Because they were great souls, their spiritual eyes caught glimpses of the life that would be, and that vision of beauty sustained them in all their challenges and lessons. They realized that the fulfillment of spiritual evolution would one day come to be, and so they raised their children to service. Though they were opposed and ridiculed by those they came to help, their work lived on, even as the work that is being done today by countless people, such as this, will live on, though I and the others will be forgotten. The power of Spirit has been launched in the world, and the children of the Directions are embracing the mighty tide.

No problem was ever solved with bloodshed. Fighting is needless and leads nowhere. We are learning to use the reason that Spirit has given us. We are opening to the message of Spirit, the realization of spiritual truths, the knowledge that there are spiritual laws and guidance from both above and within. In our perplexity we are learning where to find comfort and guidance and help. Sacred Universal Laws that had been forgotten are being revealed, and we are rediscovering those powers of the Spirit that bring us new hope and new life. In perplexity, with all the old standards being discarded, all authority questioned and its power waning, Spirit is revealed through Sacred Universal Laws, which never fail and never err. We learn to order our lives in accordance with those laws. Peace and concord rule.

These things are part of true purpose that we all work toward so that we may feed the hungry, discover fact in myth, and embody that which is precious, which is enshrined in all of us—the great truths of Spirit, long overlaid with the imaginations of the children of the Directions.

The power of Spirit—which inspired those in days gone by, which gave them vision and courage, enthusiasm and desire to serve—is available today as we look for it in the operation of those Sacred Universal Laws that are at our disposal.

The truth of Spirit abides forever. Yes, we see confusion and chaos, but this dissipates as the clear light of Spirit penetrates. And the illuminating ray is growing in strength.

Darkness is replaced by light. Ignorance is replaced by knowledge. Superstition is replaced by wisdom. Creed is replaced by the living truth of Spirit. We are free, children of freedom. It is good; we have a path we can tread. We are not helpless—there are signs of encouragement. We are free and know where our freedom will lead.

We listen to the guidance that comes to us. We are concerned with the message.

Our purpose is to seek to reveal truth, knowledge, and wisdom. The seal of truth stamps these words. No names, authorities, books—only reason.

We demand nothing that is contrary to intelligence. We

say nothing that is untrue, that is undignified, that is ignoble, that debases anyone. We seek to reveal that which elevates the whole of All Our Relations and gives a true concept of position in life and in the universe, a true concept of relationship to Spirit, and an understanding of kinship with all members of the vast universal family.

Sacred reason we appeal to. Our truth is stamped with divine purpose. Take what resonates within your heart.

We appeal to the highest and the best instincts. We only seek to dispel illusion and to bring the truth that is prized. What we believe must be founded on truth, and we seek to discard all that will not stand in the light of reason.

I strive not to lose these truths.

In this time, the application of these truths in their ramification in our daily lives has averted fearful catastrophes that had been looming in front of us.

We restore reason. We replace illusion with truth, superstition with knowledge, darkness with light so that those who are weak and struggle may find strength and those who are helpless may become whole again, so that those who are tired may become refreshed, so that those who suffer may be free.

We reveal these truths not only as they are known in their relation to the sacred laws of Spirit, but also to the laws of nature, for to us the world of nature is part of the universe of Spirit, and we cannot be spiritual if we are indifferent to All Our Relations. Those who serve are accounted as the great ones by us, and the service they render is not confined to helping the soul to find truth, for there is other service being rendered. There is the service of aiding those in pain, the service of speaking up for equality and responsibility in all actions, the service of preserving freedom, and the service of dispelling fear and giving the spirit in each of us a chance to express itself as Spirit desires that it should.

We are all parts of Spirit. And Spirit tells us that the Sacred Laws are here, in us, as a part of Spirit. Within us there is all the power we need to create a peaceful world. We have been given all the tools and we can choose to act in a life-affirming manner. We can work with Sacred Law.

We have chosen. We tune to the vibration of Spirit by which, through us, evolution moves forward.

The winds of change have blown through, and now comes new life. All looked bleak; we were unable to see. But now we do.

As Grandfather Sun moves through the skies, so the majesty of life comes to its fullest. Throughout the whole world there comes dreams and fulfillment.

It comes quickly as we exercise our free will. When we uplift one other, then behind us there are a thousand spirits who make our victory a greater one. No effort for good is ever lost. No desire to serve is ever wasted.

There, the ancestors walked the path, and made the way a little easier for those of us who follow. The path is worn smooth and is easy to find.

Sometimes I imagine these Ancient Ones, with tears in their eyes, watching those who realize the great opportunities we have of coming together as one. And sometimes I imagine their faces wreathed in smiles because some one individual has rendered a service that lights a new torch of hope for many.

The vibrations of the universe come nearer to Changing Mother to help push forward the Fifth World of Peace, which waits just around the corner. Sacred Laws show us how, by living according to them, the bounty of the Changing Mother can be poured forth.

There is a world of happiness, light, and plenty. Spirit provides everything, as obstacles are swept away.

We can do it. We can allow Sacred Law to work—all we have to do is allow it to work through us. Let us demonstrate in our own lives that we know the things of Spirit because the power of Spirit is in us. The teachings of the Sacred Laws and how they work lie within, rejoicing. If, between us, we in one case bring happiness where there has been unhappiness, knowledge where there was ignorance, then we have done service. We have a responsibility in our lives to try to inspire others to live so that they may know Spirit is working through them.

As we possess this knowledge of spiritualism we strike a balance. We have something that cannot be measured. We have the priceless knowledge of the truths of Spirit. We have the realization that our souls are linked with All That Is. We have learned how to respond to the vibrations of the messages that Spirit sends to guide us. In this environment the illusions of fear cannot continue. We birth the Fifth World of Peace. We find that the knowledge we have gained and the wisdom we have learned are of great value.

We do not judge anything by the apparent result. We see with the eyes of Spirit; we know that in every child there is perfection. I pray, and I encourage others to pray. I think that Spirit answers us all with opportunities to embrace happiness.

I have spoken to many. I have met many who see with the eyes of Spirit, and they have been served well by Spirit.

The tide of evolution rolls on. The Fourth World of Separation comes to an end, giving birth to the Fifth World of Peace. The labor has begun. But do not think labor is stress free. There are lessons yet to be learned. There will be many opportunities for healing and growth.

We build as we release our illusions. We examine the foundations of personal and spiritual collective truth. The truths of Spirit are emerging and we are building the foundations for the Fifth World, a world where the laws of Spirit play their proper part. The nearer peace gets, the more we will realize the wonder to be had.

Heron's Way of Healing

'*Auku'u*, Ancient Heron, Keeper of Knowledge, guide my heart and bless my tongue with words of hope and love. Grandfather, may I speak only with reverence. Hear my prayer that others remember Sacred Law.

Shíí shi Okahí Nakía, my prayer Snake of the South, be my inspiration. My dreams guide me. I take my first step toward the Dream Reality. I have sympathy for those in fear. I have compassion for others' lessons.

Shíí shi Okahí Hada'didla, my prayer Thunderbeings of the Southwest, fill me and infuse me with your glorious radiance. The power of healing is mine. All of today's opportunities are easy because I choose so. I build my life on Tlish Diyan principles. May it be a good building when my work is complete.

Shíí shi Okahí Eo'to'to, my prayer Bear of the West, send forth in a blaze of glory the declaration of my triumph, my emergence from the restrictions of all physical limitation. I need never go back again. My destiny lies in the future. I am certain the future brings all that I desire and more. I realize that past days have ended. I face each new day, the coming twenty-four hours, with hope and courage.

Shíí shi Okahí Dolee'atee, my prayer Little Ones of the Northwest, I, who have known ignorance, bigotry, and injustice, live to be a shining example of unconditional love and pure intent. The patterns I weave with my life are complex, full of intricate detail and knots. I go at my own pace, taking one stitch at a time. It is the perfect fit for my overall design. I take my lessons in stride. I accept what comes as part of Spirit's plan for my spiritual growth.

Shíí shi Okahí Tuma, my prayer Buffalo of the North, who has been an inspiration and sacred overseer of many of my incarnations, a deep breath invites the inner strength to move through me. I feel the exhilaration of Spirit's power. I know the excitement of growth and peace. I feel that Spirit's power is mine. I am able to face anything through that power.

Shíí shi Okahí Kachiñas, my prayer Master Teachers of the Northeast, liberate me from any limitation that keeps me from fulfilling my highest good. I am never given more than I, and my higher power, can handle. The flow of Spirit comes to me through many channels. I function on the spiritual plane as well as on the physical plane.

Shíí shi Okahí Itzá, my prayer Eagle of the East, who has been my teacher, guardian, and protector since time immemorial, the lessons of love increase my rapture. I dwell with Spirit at the center of my life. I keep that inner peace at the center of my being.

Shíí shi Okahí Nohwizá'yé, my prayer Ancestors of the Southeast, fill me with the desire to know and experience the hidden wisdom of the ages. A deep breath invites the inner strength to move through me. I feel the exhilaration of Spirit's power. I know the excitement of growth and peace. May I be a help to discouraged people. May I have the courage to help bring about what the weary world needs but does not know how to receive.

Shíí shi Okahí Yusn, my prayer Giver of All Life, universal teacher and bearer of truth and wisdom, be my inspiration. Depression must be coddled to maintain it. I choose to move beyond it, kicking it off my train. I enjoy the results. May I be used by Spirit to lighten many burdens. May many souls be helped through my efforts.

Shíí shi Okahí Esonkñhsendehé, my prayer Changing Mother, infuse me with all the healing energy, love, and compassion of your wondrous nature. I am grateful for my lessons today and know all is well. I reach forward and upward. May my character be changed by this reaching upward for the things of Spirit.

Shíí shi Okahí Pinu'u, my prayer I am I, I endeavor to person-ify hope and inspiration in my manner, speech, and actions. When I am uncomfortable with certain people and the feel-ings don't leave, I consider what might transmute the energy. I open myself to the way and ask to be shown the steps neces-sary. I am patient. I accept the limitless and eternal Spirit. May this power express itself in my life.

Shíí shi Okahí Bidáá, my prayer Light of All That Is, for whom I feel such great affinity, guide and sustain me in my quest for truth and creative powers. How great is my influence today! I go forth feeling love. I choose to—it guarantees an enjoyable day for me and everyone I meet. I will not be held back. I let Spirit lead me forward.

In my heart beats the Beauty Way, pulsing with each breath I take. In my thoughts burns the Eternal Fire, Spirit's light to show the way. In my soul is the Sacred Way; the power to obtain lies within. Heartbeat of Esonkñhsendehé, fire of Yusn, power of Bidáá, my connection is strong.

Daaiina. And so it is . . .

Coyote's Call and Echo to the Seven Generations

Libayé, Grandfather Coyote, I greet this day with love in my heart. I love myself today. Today I honor all of my body, mind, and heart. I cherish myself. I uplift myself through knowledge and wisdom handed down through the ages. I fill myself with gratitude for the opportunities of love that are presented. I feed my spirit by entering the silence and connecting to the light of All That Is. My heart opens and embraces all of life. My love blesses All My Relations. I greet this day with love in my heart.

Shíí shi Okahí Nakía, my prayer Snake of the South, for my purpose I am joyful. Searching within myself I patiently, trustingly, share myself with others. I am led out of disorder into order. I am led into success.

Shíí shi Okahí Hada'didla, my prayer Thunderbeings of the Southwest, I greet this day with love in my heart. The truths I receive today guide my steps. I move in peace. I do not look back. I make a fresh start each day.

Shíí shi Okahí Eo'to'to, my prayer Bear of the West, I greet this day with love in my heart. All events, all experiences are connected. The path I travel, alone and with others, brings me brighter days. I trust my path. It's right for me. I keep progressing in a positive manner. I am a part of the forces of love in the world.

Shíí shi Okahí Dolee'atee, my prayer Little Ones of the Northwest, I love all of life and all dimensions in every self-expression. A deep breath invites the inner strength to move through me. I feel the exhilaration of your power. I know the excitement of growth and peace. I accept every task as a lesson. I cannot fail because you are with me.

Shíí shi Okahí Tuma, my prayer Buffalo of the North, I take steps in this moment toward a higher frequency for myself and All My Relations. I trust my glimpses of harmony and wholeness, and I am grateful for the richness of my spirit. I have a sense of the eternal value of the work I do, not only for now but for the seven generations into the future.

Shíí shi Okahí Kachiñas, my prayer Master Teachers of the Northeast, I grow in my understanding of the power of love and its sacred purpose. There is nothing to fear. I know you. All roads are smooth. All who come in contact with me feel better for it. I am careful not to harbor things in my heart that put people off.

Shíí shi Okahí Itzá, my prayer Eagle of the East, I succeed with love in my life; your great power leads my experience. The creative power stirring in me needs recognition. Looking into another person, listening intently, elicits joy. I feel in touch with my own creative power—a lasting thrill, not a fleeting moment of happiness. I have confidence and am of good cheer. I have no fear of failure.

Shíí shi Okahí Nohwizá'yé, my prayer Ancestors of the Southeast, love unites all of life in such a way as to complete and fulfill. People follow my lead because I walk softly, humbly, and lovingly. I do not allow the judgments of others to affect me. I test things by what seems right within my heart.

Shíí shi Okahí Yusn, my prayer Giver of All Life, love joins us in one great breath. I bring joy wherever I go today. I give the gift of joy to everyone I meet. I seek happiness in doing right. I seek the pleasure that is to be found in doing the things that bring true happiness.

Shíí shi Okahí Esonkñhsendehé, my prayer Changing Mother, life is consciously linked. I touch someone, and you, Great Mother, touch me in return. I feel that you are not too far away for me to depend on for help. I feel confident of your readiness to give me the power that I need.

Shíí shi Okahí Pinu'u, my prayer I am I, I greet this day with love in my heart. I relish the joy at hand. I share my wisdom. All painful pasts brighten someone's future when openly shared. I rid myself of all fears and resentments so that peace and serenity may take their place. I sweep my life clean of negativity so that love may dwell within.

Shíí shi Okahí Bidáá, my prayer Light of All That Is, I greet this day with love in my heart. I am willing to give away my intimate self to others in trust. My strength as a person heal-ing increases as my ties of friendship increase. I faithfully keep a quiet time apart with you. I grow spiritually each day.

Changing Mother reflects beauty—color, sound, thought, action, love, wisdom. Each serves in its own way. I am a child of the universe in service to the whole. I am lovingly devoted to my purpose. *Pinu'u* (I am I).

Daaiina. And so it is . . .

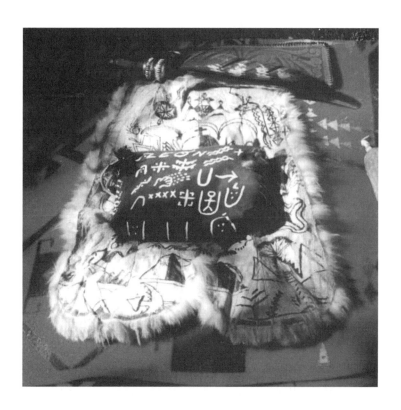

Wolf Stalking Moon

Tushi Mas, Grandmother Wolf, teacher of the path that lies within, I care, I care about all of life. All My Relations, known and unknown, seen and unseen—all vibrate with the force of creation and the will of love. I know love in a new way. My nature is that of beauty flowing through me, perceiving the presence of the Sacred Parents and being one with such a force of love.

Shíí shi Okahí Nakía, my prayer Snake of the South, this is the greatest joy! I move, change, and grow at the right pace. I trust the process. What is right for me comes to me. I let the joy of becoming warm me. It is the quality of my life that determines its value. My life is one of integrity, purity, generosity, and love.

Shíí shi Okahí Hada'didla, my prayer Thunderbeings of the Southwest, the unseen power of love opens my heart to all others and their hearts to me. I live in the present. I choose to. Gentle reminders often come. I step into my life. It is a habit I never want to break. I am a channel for your words. Your spirit flows through me into the lives of others.

Shíí shi Okahí Eo'to'to, my prayer Bear of the West, my love is my most effective tool, bringing happiness to myself and others. Today I take time to smell the flowers. Grandmother, your spirit is all about me all day long. I have no thoughts, no plans, no impulses, no emotions that you do not know about. I hide nothing from you. You see in silence, but you reward openly. I am in harmony with your divine spirit, doing my best to live the way I believe you want me to live. I am at peace.

Shíí shi Okahí Dolee'atee, my prayer Little Ones of the Northwest, I give and receive the abundance of love that is needed in my life, that I might be blessed and bless. That I am here is a wonderful mystery to which joy is the natural response. It is no accident that I am here. I persevere in all good things. I advance each day.

Shíí shi Okahí Tuma, my prayer Buffalo of the North, I know the great joy, and life is transformed. I help others face anguish. It brings us together. It softens me. It makes way for laughter. I think about other people and their paths and forget about my own. I get away from myself and I know the consolation of unselfish service to others. My experiences are useful in helping others who are where I once was.

Shíí shi Okahí Kachiñas, my prayer Master Teachers of the Northeast, I greet this day with love in my heart. Highs and lows are energy waves. They have purpose. I relax and freely flow in harmony. All that depresses me, all that I fear, is really powerless to harm me. These things are but phantoms. So I arise from fear's illusion of depression, distrust, fear, and all that hinders me in my new life. I arise to beauty, joy, peace, and work inspired by love. I arise from my death cycle to be reborn. I do not fear this rite of passage. I live and love and work with you, great teachers. Nothing hinders my new life. I seek to know more and more of this new way of living.

Shíí shi Okahí Itzá, my prayer Eagle of the East, I am soul using physical form; love calls me to life. Today and every day I have opportunities to think creatively and rely on my inner guide. I welcome the unfamiliar; I am glad for it. It moves me even closer to understanding life's mysteries. I warmly welcome all who come to me for help. I make them feel I really care.

Shíí shi Okahí Nohwizá'yé, my prayer Ancestors of the Southeast, my inner child is a personal link to the higher power of All That Is. I am conscious of the people around me. I acknowledge them and I am grateful for all they are offering me. Ancient Ones, your spirits guide me always. I rest and listen, and then I do your work.

Shíí shi Okahí Yusn, my prayer Giver of All Life, I know I am of a body. I am alert to the opportunities to share myself and cherish the freedom found. In healing I have found family and release and strength. And having found these things, the real reasons for my struggle have been taken away. Fear has no more justification in my mind. I no longer need to fight against its illusion. The struggle has just left me. I am glad that I don't have to struggle. I am glad that I don't have to fear.

Shíí shi Okahí Esonkñhsendehé, my prayer Changing Mother, I honor my body and care for it. I trust my dreams and aspirations. They are mine alone, and special to me. Achievement is possible; faith and a positive attitude ease my efforts. I help others all I can. Every searching soul that you put in my path, sacred Mother, is one for me to help. As I sincerely try to help, a supply of strength flows into me from you. My circle of helpfulness widens more and more. You nurture me with spiritual love and I pass it on to others. The more I give away the more I find for myself. That which I receive I pass on, as the circle turns.

Shíí shi Okahí Pinu'u, my prayer I am I, I bless my body. I behave the way I decide to. I choose to think about others, and to love them. I choose to forget myself. I believe in myself and release my ego-centered ways. The old ego shrivels up and dies, and upon the reborn soul my Higher Power's image becomes stamped. The elimination of ego in the growth of love for Spirit and humanity is the goal of my life. At first

I had only a faint likeness to my Divine Presence, but the picture has grown and taken on more and more of the likeness of my Higher Power until those who see me can see in me some of the power of Spirit's grace at work in my life.

Shíí shi Okahí Bidáá, my prayer Light of All That Is, the energy rises. I let serene moments wash over me. I cherish them. They soften me. The storm of lessons lightens into soft, sweet spring rain, bringing new life. I think of Spirit often. I rest in peace at the thought of Spirit's loving care.

I have known light and dark. I chose light and helped myself in a time of silence. My heart and mind have been lifted as a sacred medicine bowl in communion with my divine inner being. I received the outpouring to use in my quest for well-being of self and humanity. I am wise and humble as truth is revealed. I have found my way. I am on my path.

Daaiina. And so it is . . .

Bear's Healing Rite
of Darkness

Eo'to'to, Grandmother Bear, shower your radiant love energy upon All My Relations, calming all the elements of nature, and join me in my efforts to heal. Work with me to reclaim the beauty and perfection of my true identity. May I remember that I am *akicita* (guardian) of Sacred Law. May I walk in peace and harmony honoring all of your children.

Shíí shi Okahí Nakía, my prayer Snake of the South, fill me
and infuse me with your glorious radiance. Courage to change
accompanies faith. My fears tell me to look within to the
spiritual source of strength, ever present but often forgotten. I
come to Spirit in faith and Spirit gives me a new way of life.
This new way of life alters my whole existence, the words I
speak, the influence I have. They spring from the life within
me. I see how important is the work of a person who has this
new way of life. The words and the example of such a person
have a wide influence for the betterment of the whole.

Shíí shi Okahí Hada'didla, my prayer Thunderbeings of the
Southwest, make me a beacon for all to see so that they will
know I serve All My Relations as I use the light of Spirit to
heal, comfort, and inspire. My path is direct, clean, and love-
filled because I choose to follow my genius. I am at one with
the divine Spirit of the universe. I set my deepest affections
on things spiritual. As I think, so I am. I think of and desire
that which will help my spiritual growth. I am at one with
Spirit. No human aspiration can reach higher than that.

Shíí shi Okahí Eo'to'to, my prayer Bear of the West, I bask in
the glow of your radiance and create such a brilliant aura of
love that all I come in contact with will be blessed, and the
seeds of transformation will be planted and will come to
fruition at the proper time. The riches of a full life are easily
mine, and deservedly mine. I build up instead of tear down. I
am constructive, not destructive, in my efforts.

Shíí shi Okahí Dolee'atee, my prayer Little Ones of the
Northwest, my spirit rejoices as I spread wide my influence

in loving light. I won't be trapped by a negative attitude. I accept the challenge of turning my day around. I sometimes go aside into a quiet place of retreat with Spirit. In that place I find restoration and healing and power. I plan quiet times now and then, times when I commune with Spirit and arise rested and refreshed to carry on the work that Spirit has given me to do. I know that Spirit never gives me a load greater than I can bear. It is in serenity and peace that all true success lies.

Shíí shi Okahí Tuma, my prayer Buffalo of the North, fill me with the desire to know and experience the hidden wisdom of the ages. I bring joy wherever I go today. I give the gift of joy to everyone I meet. There is almost no work in life so hard as waiting. And yet Spirit wants me to wait. All motion is more easy than calm waiting, and yet I must wait until Spirit shows me the way. Too much activity mars my work and hinders the growth of my spiritual life. I wait patiently, preparing myself always. I am at the place I should be. Much toil and activity could not have accomplished the journey so soon.

Shíí shi Okahí Kachiñas, my prayer Master Teachers of the Northeast, as I gain true knowledge and wisdom and manifest them in my life, may I become an example and disseminator of higher truth, sharing that truth with all seekers of the Light. I turn my day around. I change the flavor of today's experiences. I lift my spirits and know all is well. I share my love, my happiness, my time, my food, my money gladly with all. I give out all the love I can with a glad and free heart and mind. I do all I can for others by Spirit and give them a royal welcome. I may never see the results of my sharing. Today they may not need me, but tomorrow may bring results from the sharing I did today.

Shíí shi Okahí Itzá, my prayer Eagle of the East, I will give comfort to those who are discouraged, and inspire those who feel defeated. I take action, even when I'm afraid; it produces growth, and without growth there is no life. Today I live! It seems, though, that when Spirit wants to express to me what it is like Spirit makes a very beautiful character. I think of a personality as Spirit's expression of character attributes. I make it as fit an expression of Spirit-like character as I can. When the beauty of a person's character is impressed upon me, it leaves an image that in turn reflects through my own actions. I look for beauty of character in those around me.

Shíí shi Okahí Nohwizá'yé, my prayer Ancestors of the Southeast, I will be a courageous example for the faint of heart and give loving succor to those who do not feel worthy of love. I listen to the music of today. I am in tune, in rhythm. I am part of the concert's beauty. Spirit is with me, to bless and help me. Spirit is all around me. I waver not in my faith or in my prayers. All power is in my partnership with Spirit. I say that to myself often and steadily. I say it until my heart sings with joy for the safety and personal power it means to me. I say it until the very force of the utterance drives back and puts to naught all the fear I may still carry. I use it as my shield of wisdom. It passes onto victory over all my created illusions, and I live a victorious life.

Shíí shi Okahí Yusn, my prayer Giver of All Life, I will honor and listen to the nudgings of Spirit and walk in the way of truth and love. Meeting, asking, resolving—all are handled with ease when least expected. Looking forward with hope, not backward, is my best effort. Spirit radiates in my life with the warmth of unconditional love. I open up like a flower to this divine tradition. I loosen my hold on self-created cares and worries. I unclasp my hold on my perception of how others should be, relax my grip, and the tide of peace and serenity flow in. I relinquish everything and receive it back again from Spirit. I do not hold onto anything so firmly that my hands are too occupied to clasp Spirit's hands as they are held out to me in love.

Shíí shi Okahí Esonkñhsendehé, my prayer Changing Mother, liberate me from any limitation that is keeping me from fulfilling my highest purpose. As I pass a friend I am grateful for her or his contribution to my wholeness. I keep balance by keeping spiritual things at the center of my life. Spirit gives me this poise and balance if I pray for it. This poise gives me power in dealing with the lives of others. This balance manifests itself more and more in my own life. I keep things in proper perspective and keep spirituality at the center of my life. I am at peace amid the distractions of everyday living.

Shíí shi Okahí Pinu'u, my prayer I am I, I assume the mantle of true identity and go forth in constant assurance of success. As I come together with friends and family I listen for Spirit's message. I hear what I need to hear because I listen. Sacred partnership and unquestioning self-love are the only conditions necessary for a spiritual life. Sacred partnership means absolute faith and trust in Spirit and the path we have created together, a belief that Spirit is the overseeing principle in the universe and that this is the intelligence and love that is the power of All That Is. Unquestioning self-love means living each day the way I believe Spirit wants us to live, constantly seeking the guidance of Spirit in every situation and being willing to do the responsible thing at all times.

Shíí shi Okahí Bidáá, my prayer Light of All That Is, I know I am a teacher of ancient wisdom and truth, now emerging. Life offers me a chance for greater happiness today; I'm growing! The rule of the Path of Beauty is order, harmony, supply, love, honesty, responsible co-creation. There is no discord on the Path of Beauty, only some things still undiscovered by the children of the Directions. The lessons of life are designed by individuals. I only lack power when I feel disconnected from Spirit and others. I succeed with Spirit as power manifests in my life.

May I never hesitate to speak my truth and share my wisdom when Spirit leads me to do so. I accept the role of a gentle guide to all those who are led to me.

Daaiina. And so it is . . .

Goose Dancing
with Thunder

Néné, Grandfather Goose, you who demonstrate endurance
in the quest for the sacred. I, who have known ignorance,
bigotry, and injustice, now ask for the strength to be a shining
example of unconditional love and pure intent. Assist me,
Néné, in my endeavors to understand and forgive. I claim the
purity of my spiritual self. May it shine radiantly for all to see
and share in its warmth. I ask you, Néné, to personify within

me the qualities of understanding, perception, and wisdom.

Shíí shi Okahí Nakía, my prayer Snake of the South, personify hope and inspiration in my manner, speech, and actions. Living life is much more than just being alive. Grandfather, help me to jump in with both feet. I know wisdom awaits me in the depths. I am molding my life, cutting and shaping my being into the essence of love and the expression of Spirit. May I recognize any fear in my desires and motives, my actions and words, and then shine light upon that shadow until it transmutes into a spiritual tool of love. As the work of molding proceeds, may I see more and more clearly what must be done to mold my life into my destiny of purpose.

Shíí shi Okahí Hada'didla, my prayer Thunderbeings of the Southwest, may I give loving assistance where needed. May the miracles continue in my life. May every day bring a miracle. I am thankful and see the miracles at work in my life and in the lives of others on this road to oneness. May my life be founded on the rock of faith. May I be disciplined in manifesting my vision.

Shíí shi Okahí Eo'to'to, my prayer Bear of the West, may I gently inspire and encourage where there is despair, speaking words of hope so all may hear. May I be fully present in this day. May I be the recipient of its gifts. There is a proper time for everything. Teach me to do things as I am ready, as conditions are right. Timing is important. May my life have balance and timing.

Shíí shi Okahí Dolee'atee, my prayer Little Ones of the Northwest, by my very presence may I bring comfort and leave in my wake an aura of peace and beauty. With a deep breath the inner strength moves through me. I feel the exhilaration of your power. I know the excitement of growth and peace. Little Ones, protect me from the illusion put forth by the shadow of fear. May I face all things through your power, which strengthens me. I have joined with my inner child—may the strength of this joy serve and protect us. May we remember that your help is always ready and available to us so that we may face anything. Little Ones, do all that is necessary for my spiritual well-being. I ask you to have your way with me.

Shíí shi Okahí Tuma, my prayer Buffalo of the North, inspire and lead me through the many unknown times. Highs and lows are energy waves. They have purpose. Help me, Grandfather, to relax and freely flow in harmony. I believe what you have in store for me is better than anything I ever could have imagined. The way to grow happily is to look for love and to give beyond that.

Shíí shi Okahí Kachiñas, my prayer Master Teachers of the Northeast, I go forth in full faith and knowledge that I am being led by my spirit. May I be a shining example for all to see. I move, change, and grow at the right pace. I trust the process. What is right for me comes to me. The joy of becoming warms me. Faith can change any situation in the field of personal relationships. I trust you to show me the way to move mountains. I am humble and know I am in partnership to create powerful, responsible acts of love. I have the faith that, together with Spirit, this is possible. Together we can move mountains. Situations change for the better.

Shíí shi Okahí Itzá, my prayer Eagle of the East, I show others that with courage and faith the impossible becomes possible, and that by releasing all attachments and foreboding I attain comfort and am blessed with abundance unending. My dreams guide me. Grandfather, I take my first step toward the Dream Reality. I have faith and believe without seeing. I am content with the results of my faith.

Shíí shi Okahí Nohwizá'yé, my prayer Ancestors of the Southeast, may I show the weak of heart that we can step off the cliff and soar among the stars. I participate in a much bigger picture than the one in my individual prayers. The big picture is being carefully orchestrated. I trust the part I have chosen to play. I am patient. It is the flow of life infinite through spirit, mind, and body that cleanses, heals, restores, and renews. I seek conscious contract with you, Ancient Ones. You are an abiding presence throughout my day. I am conscious of your help. All that I do is done in your honor and that of life infinite.

Shíí shi Okahí Yusn, my prayer Giver of All Life, with your help may I boldly carry the torch of truth and light. The mixture of calm with storm is not haphazard. Quite the contrary: growth is at the center of each. I trust its message. I ask peace and order out of world chaos. Watch over my relations. Bless them and care for them. I am grateful for the life I have been given.

Shíí shi Okahí Esonkñhsendehé, my prayer Changing Mother, may I never hesitate to step forward, whether it is to serve or to be an example of Spirit, which I now seek to embody. You and I meet today, Sacred Mother, to exchange lessons. I receive yours gladly. It is not so much what happens to me as what I make of it. I make use of my experiences to help others who are faced with the lessons I embraced. Something good comes out of my life, and the world is a better place.

Shíí shi Okahí Pinu'u, my prayer I am I, may I be your representative on the physical plane and a messenger of your essence. Change offers glad, not bad, tidings. The spiritual life depends on the unseen. I believe in the unseen and live a spiritual life. I never lose the consciousness of Spirit in me and in others. As a child in its mother's arms, I stay sheltered in the understanding and love of Changing Mother. Spirit relieves me of the weight of worry and care, misery and depression, want and woe, faintness and heartache. I open the eyes of my heart and view the glory of the unseen, more each day, in everything I see.

Shíí shi Okahí Bidáá, my prayer Light of All That Is, I dedicate my life, my energy, and all I have to the fulfillment of the promise I made before taking on physical form. I appreciate the design of my life. I draw myself close to this moment. I take in the great venture of belief. My vision is not blocked by intellectual pride.

Sacred Parents and All My Relations, my greatest desire is to fulfill my sacred purpose on this earthwalk. May my life be received as a gift of truth, honor, and generosity, standing fast as the dream becomes manifest reality.

Daaiina. And so it is . . .

Buffalo's Sacred Circle of Dance

Tuma, Grandfather Buffalo, teach me to be a representative
of the truth and wisdom that is being poured forth upon the
Changing Mother and humanity. Help me to dedicate myself
as a voice of the future and a conduit of the healing energy
from the balanced love of All That Is. May all I do and be

contribute to the manifestation of the Fifth World of Peace. May I be a warrior of peace.

Shíí shi Okahí Nakía, my prayer Snake of the South, you have been my teacher, guardian, and protector since time immemorial. I am grateful for the experiences that give my tapestry its beauty. Like a tree, I am pruned of a lot of dead branches as I become ready to bear good fruit. I think of changed people as trees that have been stripped of their old branches, pruned, cut and bare. But through the dark and seemingly dead branches flows silently, secretly, the new sap, until with the sun of spring comes new life. There are new leaves, new buds, blossoms, and fruit many times better because of the pruning. I am in the hands of *Tubaa-jish-chihenne*, Child of Water, who makes no mistakes in pruning.

Shíí shi Okahí Hada'didla, my prayer Thunderbeings of the Southwest, help me to claim peace and harmony for myself and to convey the beauty of my loving nature to all those I meet. When I am uncomfortable with certain people and the feelings don't leave, I consider what might transmute the energy. I open myself to the way and ask to be shown the steps necessary. I am patient. I am unruffled, no matter what happens. I keep my emotions in check by seeking guidance. I keep calm in the face of disturbance; inner silence is necessary to stay on an even keel. I take the calm with me into the most rushed days.

Shíí shi Okahí Eo'to'to, my prayer Bear of the West, may I go forth in knowledge that I am a being of great purpose and that each day brings me the opportunity to use and manifest my true spiritual essence. I listen to the music of today. I am in tune, in rhythm. I am part of the concert's beauty. I do each day what I can to develop spiritually and to help others to do so too. Spirit brings lessons to me to train me in divine will. I want Spirit's will for myself above all else. I spend time in the silence with Spirit every day and gain the strength I need.

Shíí shi Okahí Dolee'atee, my prayer Little Ones of the Northwest, send forth in a blaze of glory the declaration of my triumphant emergence from the restrictions of all limitations. I strengthen my supports, my connection to others, for the success of each of us. I express my love and assure my loved ones that they are needed. We surge ahead with new life. All is fundamentally well. It means that Spirit lives in my sacred space and that there is a purpose for the world, which is evolving right on course. I am not upset by circumstances but feel deeply secure in the fundamental goodness and purpose in the universe.

Shíí shi Okahí Tuma, my prayer Buffalo of the North, assist me in assuming the full mantle of my dynamic power and authority. Combined, we are one big orchestra. The conductor reads the music and directs the movements. Being in tune with the conductor feels good. I call it happiness. I play my part with joy. I remember that the first quality of greatness is service. In a way, Spirit is the greatest servant of all, because Spirit is always waiting for us to call for assistance in all endeavors of love. Spirit's strength is always available to me. I ask for it through my own free will. It is a free gift. I sincerely seek for it. A life of service is the finest life I can live. I am here on the sacred Changing Mother to serve others. That is the beginning and the end of my real worth.

Shíí shi Okahí Kachiñas, my prayer Master Teachers of the
Northeast, I am a warrior of peace. Help me to be a shining
example and inspiration to others. Opportunities to react are
many. I pause, determine the action I feel best about, and take it.
My emotional healing gets a booster shot each time I make a
responsible choice. I strive for a friendliness and helpfulness that
affect all who come near to me. I see something to love in each
of them. I welcome them, bestow little courtesies and understandings on them, and help them when they ask for help. I
send no one away without a word of cheer, a feeling that I really
care about them. Spirit put the impulse in someone's mind to
come to me. I assure them a warm welcome.

Shíí shi Okahí Itzá, my prayer Eagle of the East, world teacher
and bearer of truth and wisdom, be my inspiration. In the
moment lives Spirit within. In the moment I am creative,
blessed with gifts like no others. I stay in the moment and offer
those gifts, guided by Spirit's will. I am, therefore I can. To
accomplish much, I am much. In all cases, doing is the expression of being. I am honest, pure, generous, and loving. I choose
the positive and keep choosing it, and I am used by Spirit to
accomplish many things worthwhile. I am given opportunities
because I am ready for them. Entering the silence with my
Higher Power is my daily preparation for creative action.

Shíí shi Okahí Nohwizá'yé, my prayer Ancestors of the
Southeast, may I bring forth hidden truths and the higher
wisdom of Spirit in such a way that it can be understood by
all who seek to know. Today, I take time to smell the flowers.
Spirit works through me because I do not hurry. I go very
slowly, very quietly from one duty to the next, taking time to

rest and pray between. I take everything in order. I venture
often into the rest of Spirit and find peace. All work results
from resting with Spirit. I claim the power to work miracles in
human lives. I can do many things through my Higher Power.
I do good things through Changing Mother, who renews me
and gives me strength. I partake regularly of rest and prayer.

Shíí shi Okahí Yusn, my prayer Giver of All Life, be my guiding
light and inspiration; teach me discernment and to give wise
counsel to those who are led to me. Every day is a gift-giving
time because I make it so. I have faith's look. By faith I look
beyond the now into the infinite.

Shíí shi Okahí Esonkñhsendehé, my prayer Changing Mother, I
seek a clear connection as the more I know the more I may
give, the more I receive of your precious love. I exercise my
power to act and feel the fullness of my being. Peace is the
gift Spirit gives in the midst of this transitional world. To
know Spirit's peace is to be embraced in the unconditional
love of the Sacred Parents. I have earned that peace I follow:
the Path of the Heart, the Path of Beauty, the Sacred
Universal Laws of Love.

Shíí shi Okahí Pinu'u, my prayer I am I, infuse me with all
the healing energy, love, and compassion of your wondrous
nature. I don't wait to be loved. I love others fully. I know
that I, too, am loved. I feel it. I know unconditional love. I
face the future with courage. I am given strength to walk my
path fearlessly.

Shíí shi Okahí Bidáá, my prayer Light of All That Is, allow me
to be a nurturer and healer of all those who seek comfort,

hope, and inspiration. I am alert to the opportunities to share myself and cherish the freedom found. I believe that Spirit's grace has saved me. I believe that Spirit means to heal me yet more and to keep me on the Path of Beauty. I depend on Spirit.

Sacred Parents, allow me to be the instrument by which All My Relations attain wholeness in body, mind, and spirit. May all who I meet and serve be infused with balance, peace, and harmony.

Daaiina. And so it is . . .

Condor Crossing

E'o, Great Thunderbird, looking back, I am filled with gratitude. Looking forward, I am filled with hope. Looking upward, I am aware of my strength. Looking inward, I find peace.

Shíí shi Okahí Nakía, my prayer Snake of the South, I celebrate today. Today holds a special promise for me. I am in harmony. I share with others. My courage strengthens others, and others strengthen me. I continually remind myself that I

71

am not perfect—no one is. I lay to rest the unrealistic expectations that I visualize for myself. I am worthy just as I am.

Shíí shi Okahí Hada'didla, my prayer Thunderbeings of the Southwest, I find a moment to reflect on my abilities and talents and I use them to better the world. I accept responsibility for my actions, not for the outcome of a situation; that is all that is asked of me. It is one of the assignments of life, and homework is forthcoming. I cherish my own uniqueness and recognize the uniqueness of others. In accepting myself, I live in harmony with others.

Shíí shi Okahí Eo'to'to, my prayer Bear of the West, I choose to be rid of anxiety and stress. That I am here is a wonderful mystery to which joy is the natural response. It is no accident that I am here. I refrain from speaking unkind words about other people. I do not cause another to be hurt by thoughtless speech.

Shíí shi Okahí Dolee'atee, my prayer Little Ones of the Northwest, I remain calm so I may better handle the lessons I face today. Each and every expression of love I offer makes smooth another step I take in life. I am responsible for my words and actions. May they reflect love and gentleness toward others.

Shíí shi Okahí Tuma, my prayer Buffalo of the North, I make the most of today—yesterday cannot be relived and tomorrow is a welcome, and unknown, adventure. Every person, every situation, adds to my success. My attitude helps others succeed too. I give myself the gift of personal time. A moment of peace and quiet is the best gift I can give myself.

Shíí shi Okahí Kachiñas, my prayer Master Teachers of the Northeast, when I become too focused on myself may I remember how important my friends and loved ones are to me. Today and every day I pray for the wisdom to choose wise counselors and the strength to love and heal myself. There are times when I worry too much about things I cannot control. I actively guide my thoughts toward positive outcomes, eliminating stress over things that may never come to pass.

Shíí shi Okahí Itzá, my prayer Eagle of the East, my life would be empty without the gift of your companionship. Life is a process. I accept the variations with gratitude. Each in its own way blesses me. Each of us has two ends—one for thinking, one for sitting. Our success depends on when we use each.

Shíí shi Okahí Nohwizá'yé, my prayer Ancestors of the Southeast, I greet this day with optimism and energy. I am on a path to full understanding. I learn to trust the lifeline offered by my healing and by Spirit and my friends. As I learn, my footing is less tentative and it supports me more securely. I celebrate work. I take pride in what I do, no matter how small the task. I do the best I can and am satisfied with myself.

Shíí shi Okahí Yusn, my prayer Giver of All Life, I do not allow others to shape my actions because of their behavior. I anticipate with faith. All experiences carry me forward to fulfill my goal in life. I am alert to the nudge. I celebrate the love and support I receive from others. I make time to show my appreciation and include others in my successes.

Shíí shi Okahí Esonkñhsendehé, my prayer Changing Mother, I celebrate today by encouraging others to be joyful. I am free. No one controls my actions. Spirit gives the only approval that counts. Aligning my will with Spirit's will guarantees personal freedom. I greet this day ready to take control of my behavior and my attitude. My day is as good as I make it.

Shíí shi Okahí Pinu'u, my prayer I am I, I celebrate all that is good in my life. I invite blessings. I also shower blessing on my friends. Sometimes I react to times of high stress by becoming indifferent. I become more aware of when I push others away and instead express my needs for time alone.

Shíí shi Okahí Bidáá, my prayer Light of All That Is, I am proud of the goals I have achieved. I let another in, and feel the rush of happiness. When I know a rough day is ahead I plan for ways to boost my energy. Exercise, proper nutrition, and a positive outlook strengthen me. I make time for myself.

Echicasay, All My Relations, I celebrate that I am capable of doing good for myself and you.
Daaiina. And so it is . . .

Hummingbird's Quest
for the Sacred

Tocha, Grandmother Flower Eagle, grant my family
strength and long life. I would have these things before I
would have my own life.

Shíí shi Okahí Nakía, my prayer Snake of the South, thank
you for all you have given me. Even if it takes effort, I smile
at others. Both are better for it. I am thankful for the place

I have to come at the end of a hectic day. I make a place for my spirit and body to be refreshed.

Shíí shi Okahí Hada'didla, my prayer Thunderbeings of the Southwest, I thank you for the victories, for the strength. I look at each moment with childish eyes. I find joy and contentment. I celebrate all the choices that are before me this day. I strive to be open to all possibilities, seeking to use my talents in new ways.

Shíí shi Okahí Eo'to'to, my prayer Bear of the West, now I ask that you grant me the true sight that I might see clearly what is before me. My understanding of Spirit and the power of that presence is proportionate to my faith in that power. Not unlike the power of electricity, I plug into the Source for the light of understanding and for the strength to see my way. When I am weary and feel like I just cannot go on, I look for inspiration from those I trust for support. I gather strength from their belief in me.

Shíí shi Okahí Dolee'atee, my prayer Little Ones of the Northwest, may I ever be strong enough to recognize our connection. My imagination serves me today. It offers me ideas and the courage I need to go forth. Anger has blocked my ability to be productive. When I was stuck dwelling on hostile feelings I alienated myself from others. Now I strive for harmony and cooperation.

Shíí shi Okahí Tuma, my prayer Buffalo of the North, may I always stand tall where I walk yet be ever mindful that all light comes from the brilliance of Grandfather Sun's smile. There is nothing to fear. I know Spirit. All roads are smooth. An efficient person chooses the responsible way to do the job; an effective person chooses the responsible job. I strive to be both.

Shíí shi Okahí Kachiñas, my prayer Master Teachers of the Northeast, only by trying something new do I experience the satisfaction of action on my own inner strength and motivation. I came to say a word and I shall say it now. I exercise my power to act and feel the fullness of my being. I am adventuresome and do things I have never tried.

Shíí shi Okahí Itzá, my prayer Eagle of the East, if death prevents me, these words will be said by tomorrow, for tomorrow never leaves a secret in the book of eternity. The truths I receive today guide my steps. I move in peace. I celebrate the child within today and take time to play. Laughter and play do not mean being irresponsible. Humor gives me the strength to continue.

Shíí shi Okahí Nohwizá'yé, my prayer Ancestors of the Southeast, I came to live in the glory of love and in the light of beauty, which are reflections of Yusn. I have opportunities every day to still my mind. The messages I need come quickly. My answers are within. Teaching seekers of the path in today's world seems so difficult. It takes a loving but firm intent, time to listen, and words of encouragement for teacher and student alike.

Shíí shi Okahí Yusn, my prayer Giver of All Life, I am here, living, and I cannot be neutral in the energy of life, for through my living word I leave my pure intent and vibration.

My prayer has given me this new option. It guarantees every hurdle is lightened. The knowledge that joy is inherent within every experience is mine, now and forever. My friendships are special gifts. I spend time nurturing my relationships with my friends and seek out their company.

Shíí shi Okahí Esonkñhsendehé, my prayer Changing Mother, I came here to be for all and with all, and what I do today will be echoed by many. The truths I receive today guide my steps. I move in peace. I am a person who looks for the qualities in others that make them special and unique. I recognize that no two people are exactly alike—yet all are deserving of the same amount of respect.

Shíí shi Okahí Pinu'u, my prayer I am I, what I say now with my heart will be said by a thousand hearts. Today I do something I've been putting off. A whole collection of somedays lay the groundwork for the person I build within. I give myself permission to relax today. My world will not come apart if I pause to refresh my spirit. I can control how much pressure I place on myself and I can control my response to that pressure.

Shíí shi Okahí Bidáá, my prayer Light of All That Is, what blind joy, what hunger to use up the air that I breathe; all parts of my being rejoice. I cherish every moment today. Each one is special and will not visit me again. I am happier when I choose to do things rather than feeling I have to do them. I have control over my tasks and do not let any moment control me. I am responsible for shaping my day.

Sacred Parents, what biting itch to spend absolutely all of myself in one single burst of laughter. *Ukehé*, thank you, my parents. Thank you for my life!

Daaiina. And so it is . . .

nohwizá'yé zhiheego
Living in the Way
of the Ancestors

We are now in the midst of transition. As always happens before birth, there is labor. The birth of the Fifth World of Peace means transition and effort. As the Fifth World comes there will be "growing pains."

But there has been planted in our world a seed that is growing, and the efforts to nurture the seed have been successful. The prophecies have foretold of this time. It is happening even as I write these words.

There are many big changes taking place. There have been breakups and there have been upheavals. Many consider this to be a time of darkness and difficulty. Many say "Things are worse." But there is behind all this a power that is making for the evolution of this world.

Many of us have seen, or are now seeing, the world as it shall be. That concept we try to relay to those who are receptive, to inspire them to go on with their work. The images I have been shown tell me it is only a matter of time.

As the children of the Directions come together we recognize that all politics, religion, science, and knowledge are part of one whole. As we heal and embrace our true identity as responsible co-creators, pain, sorrow, fear, mourning, and unhappiness dissipate and our world moves toward becoming a place of smiles and happy laughter. The greatest teacher in our world today is one who can work to lift the sorrows of others and make the lives of others better.

The old Fourth World was characterized by a paradigm in which when one individual had something he tried to keep it for himself instead of using it to help others. In time a system was created that is now collapsing because its foundations were irresponsible in relation to the whole.

As people develop their gifts, which all come from Spirit, and use those gifts for the benefit of All Our Relations, we build a system founded on that which is eternal and based in love.

These are not new things that I am telling you. They are the old, old truths that those who have seen with the eyes of Spirit have taught for many centuries. But until this time the shadow of fear's hold over humanity's reason was too strong; now we are shown that we are learning the lessons of Spirit.

We are moving forward in our evolution as we get back to Spirit and Sacred Law. The Fifth World of Peace is birthing. I can see how prophecies are coming to fulfillment.

We are learning that the bounty of the sacred Changing Mother must be properly divided among All Our Relations. We are reevaluating to determine the most responsible way to divide the things we have among all who are here. Is this not a simple life concept?

We are breaking down vested interests. Sacred Laws are perfect. If we live our own lives seeking only to serve others, then Spirit operates through us. That applies to me and to you and to All Our Relations. It is possible, for it is the way. Sacred Law is perfect and we cannot cheat it. We learn the Laws and put them into operation.

The light of Spirit is penetrating the darkness that once was, and out of the chaos and disorder there is being built the Fifth World of Peace, a world in which there is no inequality, no injustice, no division of those who have too much and those who have too little, a world in which all the gifts will be divided and all the bounty will be evenly shared.

I do not care by what name you call the dawn of this time, but it is the Fifth World of Peace, as I was taught and shown, that is coming into fulfillment, accompanied by co-creative power with Spirit and the service of all faithful hearts who seek but to bring new joy, new life, new happiness to the sacred Changing Mother.

Sometimes you may think that your work is being held back, but all the time instruments are being used by people in all places without their knowledge, instruments unknown even to themselves. The Sacred Parents support our evolution. Destruction is thwarted by compassion and responsible action. That is why I urge you again and again to embrace your connection, your power, your purpose of service. What you name this work, this time, this power I care not. It goes on. We all work together. It moves forward.

I am proud that because of our efforts we have accomplished so much throughout our world. Hearts that were once sad are now a little more joyful. Light has pierced the gloom of darkness. Now there is more knowledge where before there was ignorance. We have aided those who had become fainthearted, given strength to those who were weary, guided those who had lost their way, and acted as an incentive to those who strive to work for All Our Relations, giving them the realization that behind them there is a mighty support system of love spurring them on in all their endeavors for the Sacred Parents and All Our Relations.

I am happy that I can bring you insight into what lies beyond, so that you may realize more than you ever did before that you have never lost your loved ones, that death does not divide but brings together those who love and affection and friendship have made one in heart and soul.

I wish you could see the extent of our work's influence throughout the world. Together, you and I have helped to break barriers, to remove obstacles, and to bring knowledge. These are the things our world needs, the simple truths that enable spiritual, mental, and physical freedom to reign supreme. As you know, we live to serve, for through service and service alone do we evolve.

I want to remind you all once again that I am the same as you. I am only one of many seeking to bring forth the truth, the simple truth of Spirit, the realization that we are all parts of the web of life. Spirit is within us. We have a sacred heritage and are entitled to all the bounty of the Sacred Parents because of our latent sacredness, and all obstacles and institutions that have stood in the way of that fullness are being swept away. Our labor is not only to free our souls and minds, but to free our bodies too.

That is the task to which we have dedicated ourselves. That is the service we strive to perform. If I, as an instrument, am privileged to bring those truths to others and help, then I rejoice. I have worked for some time and I continue to work so that through our united efforts we may bring growth—growth that is essential—into our world. We have the knowledge, we have the truth, we have the responsibility that comes with all knowledge of using it so that we are greater instruments.

Remember always, when we are questioned, that the hall-mark of sacred truth is stamped on the message of love because we appeal only to reason. The message that is in this time is one that does not debase us, that does not demean our intelligence, that does not seek to turn us from the Path of Beauty, goodness, or service. Rather, it strives to make us realize our latent sacredness so that, conscious of our own tie with Spirit, we may so order our lives that the Sacred Parents are expressed in all that we do.

Great work is being achieved by all those conscious of spiritual truths banding together and using our power to dissipate the fog of darkness that once ruled the Fourth World of Separation. Go forward with great confidence, knowing that all the forces of good, helpfulness, and service are at your side.

There is a great field for service in front of us all. We look forward with joyful anticipation to the fact that we are able to help many who do not know where to turn, who do not trust any more the faith of yesterday, and who search for the truth that withstands the questioning. We bring them to knowledge of spiritual truth and spiritual law. We seek to remind them of their own innate powers of spirituality, to help them understand the co-creative power that is theirs, so that they may sweep away forever the ideas of cringing self-victimization.

We seek to make our world realize the great power of Spirit, waiting to co-create with all those who strive to serve All Our Relations, so that, armed with knowledge, we can fight all illusions of fear and allow the light of spiritual truth to radiate its glorious beams. That is our task. And we bring with us that power of the Sacred Parents that can inspire and guide, can uphold and sustain, can bring food to hungry minds and healing to bodies racked with pain, that can bring inspiration and revelation, truth and wisdom for all.

We can fill our lives with this power just as we are provided with the capacity to understand and receive it. We seek to co-create with all who desire to raise the vibration of this time.

Flicker Dancing in the Light

Nanpenape, Red Shaft, protect us from all negative thoughts. *Pinu' Echicasay,* I am All My Relations. We are mighty. May we never give up on our dreams. May we love one another and shower all with affection.

Chajala Nakía, healing Snake of the South, I am noble by birth and infinite lineage. I share our likeness and relish whatever differences surface. The chain of friendship I've created makes me the proud owner of wholeness. I am succeeding, moving forward with courage and self-awareness on this, my Path of Beauty. It is impossible to take back harsh words spoken in anger. Today I think before I speak, choosing my words responsibly, for I must live with them too.

Chajala Hada'didla, healing Thunderbeings of the Southwest, the mountains, the trees, the rivers change their appearance with time and seasons, as I change with my experiences and emotions. I am grateful for my lessons today and know all is well. Every hour of this day is mine. I choose to celebrate each moment with a glad heart. Whatever I do this day, I try to do with enthusiasm. Joy brings more joy.

Chajala Eo'to'to, healing Bear of the West, the lofty poplar that resembles a bride in the daytime will look like a column of smoke in the evening; prayer and meditation direct my efforts today. My purpose is fulfilled. My heart feels for those who suffer. I make an effort to ease another's pain and reach out to those who are in need.

Chajala Dolee'atee, healing Little Ones of the Northwest, the huge rock that stands impregnable at noon will appear small at night, with Changing Mother for his bed and the sky for his cover; I may run into some stone people today. I pick up only those lessons that are mine. I celebrate and welcome the changes in my life, whether they are big or small. Without change I would not grow.

Chajala Tuma, healing Buffalo of the North, the rivulet that I see glittering in the morning and hear chanting of eternity will, in the evening, turn to a stream of cleansing tears washing my soul. I am in control of my attitude. Today is what I longed for. I can say yes to today and all that it brings. I find peace in the gifts of the present moment.

Chajala Kachiñas, healing Master Teachers of the Northeast, the appearance of things change according to the emotions; thus, all the strength I need is at hand. I let go and let Spirit help me. I will not dwell in the past and relive old hurts. Today is a glorious new beginning. With each new day I am given the opportunity to be strengthened by my past, not burdened by it.

Chajala Itzá, healing Eagle of the East, I see magic and beauty in all things, as the magic and beauty are truly within me. Self-pity could beckon. Fortunately, I have other choices. Every day I am faced with lessons. I embrace them. I do what needs to be done and complete my lessons.

Chajala Nohwizá'yé, healing Ancestors of the Southeast, the purpose of Spirit in my heart is concealed, and each day is a training ground. Every experience trains me to recognize the value of succeeding experiences. With richness I develop, one moment at a time. I accept that this day may bring me many varying emotions. I find what strengthens me in each experience and greet whatever lies ahead.

Chajala Yusn, healing Giver of All Life, outer appearances cannot be judged. Through the confusion comes a hand reaching toward me, pulling me forward, securing my place in the universal family. Dominance and coercion are not tools of effective cooperation. Proper training, positive feedback, and genuine concern facilitate healing and growth.

Chajala Esonkñhsendehé, healing Changing Mother, the art of my life is a direct communication between my imagination and the visions you give. Each moment is a chance to know better who I am and to understand the real contribution I make in this life. The anticipation of my ideas excites me. Recognizing another's accomplishments heightens their self-esteem and increases healing. Today I praise my associates' success.

Chajala Pinu'u, healing Higher Power of I am I, my imagination roams wide and far. I know Spirit's will when I listen to my inner voice. I do what feels right, and peace is always my reward. Life is like a river. There are times of calm and times of rough rapids and strong undercurrents. I equip my raft with many oars to guide me through rough waters.

Chajala Bidáá, healing Light of All That Is, I live my life as a creative expression of my sacred purpose. I let my healing shine its light in my life. My monsters flee. As I am bombarded by the views of the world I refrain from engaging in unneeded and unnecessary exchanges of energy just to make a status statement.

Sacred Parents, we have created each other. Imagination is the creator; its nearest and clearest manifestation is All My Relations. Yes, life is creative art. I am pleased with our creation.
    Daaiina. And so it is . . .

Hawk's Living Your Vision

Kelei, Red-tailed Brother, may the many faiths that humanity professes find within their meaning the one commonality known as love. May I always see my path through the valley of beliefs. Freedom is the gift of personal truth. May I always recognize mine.

Chajala Nakía, healing Snake of the South, Beauty is my religion. I worship her as my Spirit; I have opportunities every day to still my mind. The messages I need come quickly. My answers are within me. I pray that I may fulfill my purpose in life. I pray that I may be used as an instrument of unconditional love in the world.

Chajala Hada'didla, healing Thunderbeings of the Southwest, Beauty is the visible, manifest, and perfect handiwork of co-creation. One step, one moment, the next step and its moment. How simple life can bring freedom! I am one with those who gather together. I feel the strength of a consecrated circle.

Chajala Eo'to'to, healing Bear of the West, I believe in the sacredness of Beauty that is at once the beginning of my worship of life. I go within if ever I feel dissatisfied. I find my joy there, and my sense of well being, and that Sacred Law is in charge. I lift my eyes from their former position of down-cast. I set my sights on higher ground.

Chajala Dolee'atee, healing Little Ones of the Northwest, Beauty is the source of my nurturing happiness. Today I take time to smell the flowers. I pray that I may have a seeing eye. I pray that with the eye of faith I may see Spirit's purpose everywhere.

Chajala Tuma, healing Buffalo of the North, I stand before Beauty and forgive myself for my illusions of fear. I get free. I tackle this small task today. It blesses me in special ways. I am strong in Spirit's strength. I trust Spirit to guide me on the path.

Chajala Kachiñas, healing Master Teachers of the Northeast, Beauty brings my heart closer to true identity today. I pay particular attention to the accomplishments of others—those close to me, and those I read or hear about. I believe their example and feel the forward push. Love embraces fear and transmutes anguish in my life. I pray that others can know the peace that love brings.

Chajala Itzá, healing Eagle of the East, Beauty is the mirror of my affections and the teacher of my heart in the ways of nature. Today, I take my first few baby steps. I choose responsibly. I forgive others as I am forgiven.

Chajala Nohwizá'yé, healing Ancestors of the Southeast, Beauty is my life's home. In the moment lives Spirit within. In the moment I am creative, blessed with gifts like no others. I stay in the moment and offer those gifts, guided by Spirit's will. I am truly thankful on this day. I bring my gifts and lay them on the altar of humanity's heart.

Chajala Yusn, healing Giver of All Life, my spirit understands Beauty and today invites me to grow, to move beyond my present self. It offers me chances to be the person I always dreamed of being. I am courageous. I am not alone. I travel my path with faith, prayer, and hope. I carry good things into the adventure that lies ahead.

Chajala Esonkñhsendehé, healing Changing Mother, I live and grow with Beauty. Combined we are one big orchestra. The conductor reads the music and directs the movements. Being in tune with the conductor feels good. I call it happiness. I play my part with joy. Spirit, as I understand that power, guides me one day at a time in my life. Each day Spirit supplies the wisdom and strength that I need.

Chajala Pinu'u, healing Higher Power of I am I, even though I am unable to describe Beauty in words, my relationships with others are as healthy and fulfilling as my communication with Spirit. I realize that, positive or negative, past days have ended. I face each new day, the coming twenty-four hours, with hope and courage.

Chajala Bidáá, healing Light of All That Is, Beauty is a sensation that my eyes cannot see. I strengthen my supports, my connection to others, for the success of All My Relations. I express my love and assure my loved ones that they are needed. We surge ahead with new life. I understand my real wants and needs. Spirit grants me the capacity for honesty, unselfishness, and love.

Echicasay, All My Relations, Beauty is derived from both the one who observes and the one who is looked upon. True Beauty is a ray that emanates from the most sacred of sacred and illuminates the body, as life comes from the depths of the Changing Mother and gives color and scent to a flower.

Daaiina. And so it is . . .

Deer Dancing the Shadow

Chuchip, Gentle Deer, guardian of unconditional love,
what shall be my destiny? I am one with All My Relations.
I ponder day and night on my place and identity, and I am
intoxicated with my tears of joy.

Chajala Nakía, healing Snake of the South, one hour devoted
to the pursuit of Beauty—one step, one moment, the next
step and its moment. How simple life can bring freedom! It is

wise to speak of Spirit, whom we cannot understand, and each other, whom we endeavor to understand.

Chajala Hada'didla, healing Thunderbeings of the Southwest, love is full within its glory. Today has a clarity about it that I appreciate. I know who I am. I know what I believe. I act accordingly. I know that I am the breath and fragrance of Spirit.

Chajala Eo'to'to, healing Bear of the West, I give to those who are frightened my strength. Today I let my excitement for life's possibilities spur me on. I am Spirit in leaf, in flower, and oftentimes in fruit.

Chajala Dolee'atee, healing Little Ones of the Northwest, I see All My Relations in their glory as I gift myself some time alone. I deserve that gift today and every day. To not take my time to enter the silence is a sign of fear.

Chajala Tuma, healing Buffalo of the North, with you I stand acclaiming your majesty. Rewards are forthcoming because I am honest. The love in me freely flows while time undulates awhile, then breaks the illusion, revealing the truth of the no-time.

Chajala Kachiñas, healing Master Teachers of the Northeast, I sing praises of your great deeds. I take today in my arms and love it. I love all it offers; it is my friend bearing gifts galore. Look down on me: I am the manifestation of Spirit's creation.

Chajala Itzá, healing Eagle of the East, I smile at others today even if I'm a little under the weather. Both are better for it. I am devoted to loving All My Relations. Be ever watchful over our welfare and zealous in our success.

Chajala Nohwizá'yé, healing Ancestors of the Southeast, I gaze upon you as the manifestation of prophecy. Each step taken is in harmony with my higher power. I experience nothing alone. I breathe in and tap the plentiful source of strength: the eternal Now. You, Ancient Ones, are a blessing in the tapestry of my life.

Chajala Yusn, healing Giver of All Life, my spirit exudes even to the canopy of heaven. I smile at others today even if I don't feel like it. Both are better for it. I seek happiness in my time of silence; as I draw close I hear my soul whisper to my heart, saying "The happiness you seek is born and reared in the depths of your heart and emerges with Spirit's embrace."

Chajala Esonkñhsendehé, healing Changing Mother, behold, I find you in my time alone. I do not turn my back on joy. I am glad for all of life's experiences. The panorama inspires me fully. When I open my heart to find happiness I discover in its domain happiness mirrored, my inner child cradled in raiment joy, and my purpose is there.

Chajala Pinu'u, healing Higher Power of I am I, standing by your side I stretch my hand in every direction as opportunities to share my secrets present themselves. I am courageous. Happiness is the truth I seek, its manifestation like a river speeding to the plain; on its arrival, joyous emergence joins the sea.

Chajala Bidáá, healing Light of All That Is, I receive love and kindness from your invisible source—I cherish every moment. Each one is special and will visit me no more. For I am happy in my aspirations to my quest; when I attain my goal, I fly long and high in my vantage.

Sacred Parents, your shelter is the warmth and love of my soul. In this moment I own my true self, calling that self by appropriate name. I taste my essence in its purity and sacredness. My heart has been cleansed. I am filled with love and the Spirit of All My Relations.

Daaiina. And so it is . . .

Puma's Journey

Tomacho, Grandmother Nightwalker, it is my higher power and spiritual guides, those of the Directions, that gather here in my circle to assist me, who heal in and through me. I am a clean conduit that they work through. The greatest and the only lasting privilege I have is that the powers and these guides are willing to work through me. What could be greater than to be Spirit's mind, eyes, ears, nose, mouth, arms, hands, legs, and feet here on Earth?

Chajala Nakía, healing Snake of the South, sometimes your spiritual power feels like energy or electricity when it is moving in and through me. There is nothing to fear. I know Spirit. All roads are made smooth. This is how I call to Spirit. I pray.

Chajala Hada'didla, healing Thunderbeings of the Southwest, spiritual power is really a distinctive kind of knowledge that is like the key that opens the door or the switch that starts the energy moving. Life offers me a chance for greater happiness; I'm growing! I smudge with sage and offer sacred pollen to the Directions in gratitude.

Chajala Eo'to'to, healing Bear of the West, spiritual power is that special insight that I need to break up a log jam of knowledge. The most important lesson I am learning, the lesson that eliminates all my pain and struggle, is receiving fully that which life offers in this moment and every moment. As my right hand extends to give to All My Relations, my left hand opens to receive the gifts I know come from Spirit and the guides of the Directions.

Chajala Dolee'atee, healing Little Ones of the Northwest, spiritual power is the prime mover; those key insights that are given to me by Spirit and the guides of the Directions. I need never go back again. I am spared that. My destiny lies in the future. I am certain it brings all that I desire and more. I close my eyes and deep breathe seven times to relax and prepare myself.

Chajala Tuma, healing Buffalo of the North, I cleanse and purify myself with smoke or water, and then let Spirit make me into a clean conduit to work me in and through for the sake of others. In this day that stands before me I am certain that I have many chances for growth, for kindness to others, for developing confidence in me. I am thoughtful in my actions. They are special and will be repeated no more. Each time I breathe I envision the air entering through my fingertips, track it up into my chest, hold it briefly, let it go, track it down my abdomen, out my legs and feet, and let it exit out my toes. I am grounded in my reality of Spirit.

Chajala Kachiñas, healing Master Teachers of the Northeast, I release all that stands in the way of achieving my full potential—doubt, guilt, reluctance, fear, selfishness, wanting to tell Spirit how and when something ought to be done. The lessons of love increase my rapture. Then I breathe seven times. I am completely relaxed and rid of any distractions that may cloud my focus of intent.

Chajala Itzá, healing Eagle of the East, I ask for personal help, but my reason is that I want to be helped so that I can help others. I am never given more than I, and my higher power, can handle. I begin to chant softly, concentrating intently upon calling Spirit and the guides of the Directions.

Chajala Nohwizá'yé, healing Ancestors of the Southeast, nothing selfish lives in my intent. I trust that all is well. I reflect on the past momentarily and know I move in the right direction. I use this time of silence and this circle of prayer to get myself out of the way of Spirit and the guides of the Directions.

Chajala Yusn, healing the Giver of All Life, Spirit's wish is that I do for others and I am taken care of. I am grateful for the experiences that give my tapestry its beauty. Knowing what the energies are in each Direction, from a human point of view, I call to those that most closely can assist in the manifestation of my prayers.

Chajala Esonkñhsendehé, healing Changing Mother, it is through community that a strong, united voice is heard. A deep breath invites the inner strength to move through me. I feel the exhilaration of Spirit's power. I know the excitement of growth and peace. Through my circle of prayer and time of silence the guides of the Directions present me with choices, and when I follow their guidance it is only a little while before I see why the guides that presented themselves chose to appear.

Chajala Pinu'u, healing I am I, this approach gives me personal satisfaction. Life offers me a chance for greater happiness today. When I close my eyes and sing, I roll my eyes up a little and look at the images provided within my head.

Chajala Bidáá, healing Light of All That Is, those who live for one another learn that love is the bond of perfect unity. I take this moment to look back at last year. I am moving forward. I continue to do so. When I concentrate on the images that present themselves in my time of silence I am freed of confusion.

Echicasay, All My Relations, when we put others ahead of ourselves there is perfect love—perfect unity—and no one has to worry about equality any more. We have something much better.

Daaiina. And so it is . . .

Parrot's Prophecy

Kyaro, Parrot Guardian of the Fifth World's Rainbow
prophecy, I came into this life by choice. I came all-knowing
to learn to remember my sacredness and seek the hidden
shadows within myself to expose them to Spirit's transmuting
light. I came as a member of a clan and tribe and belonged to
a county and town. Now I see we are one *go-tah*, one family.
The universe is my home and *Echicasay*, All My Relations, is
my tribe.

Chajala Nakía, healing Snake of the South, our bond is strong, and it is with joyous communion that I greet you. I am conscious of the people around me. I acknowledge them and I am thankful for all they are offering me. Love is my Sacred Parents, and all know love via Spirit's embrace.

Chajala Hada'didla, healing Thunderbeings of the Southwest, learning follows me on my road. One small change today: a smile at the first person I meet, entering the silence at sunset, circulating the energy of my life helps me chart a new course. I encourage another to join me. I am on my way. And so I speak of love as the image of my hopes, a glory to behold always.

Chajala Eo'to'to, healing Bear of the West, the best knowledge is a dream I hold steadfast. I look to this day. Every day is a new beginning. I was chosen by Love, and I follow Love's call.

Chajala Dolee'atee, healing Little Ones of the Northwest, what is Sacred Law? I look at each moment through the eyes of a child. I find joy and contentment. Love is the flower that grows and blossoms within my heart.

Chajala Tuma, healing Buffalo of the North, I am compelled by the law of Spirit to create dreams of peace. What a wonderful collection of invitations I have today! Love is the freedom in the world, elevating my spirit and keeping me to my course.

Chajala Kachiñas, healing Master Teachers of the Northeast, I am free; the mixture of calm with storm is not haphazard. Quite the contrary: growth is at the center of each. I trust its message. Love comes to me, robed in humility, and I embrace her to create in Spirit's name.

Chajala Itzá, healing Eagle of the East, I am an infinite child of the universe. Life offers me a chance for greater happiness—I am growing! Love that comes with my awakening grows with each embrace.

Chajala Nohwizá'yé, healing Ancestors of the Southeast, I am strong by my spirit; I take care of my inner child today. Together we face the adventure of life. Love is born and descends upon me.

Chajala Yusn, healing Giver of All Life, I have birthed on this Earth a sanctuary of peace from which I can now journey as the day invites me to grow, to move beyond my present self. It offers me chances to be the person I always dreamed of being. I am courageous. I am not alone. I lead Love's cavalcade to a bed of faithful motion. There love does grow and prosper.

Chajala Esonkñhsendehé, healing Changing Mother, I am Sacred Law and Spirit has my attention, directs my energies, and makes the most of my special talents. I am aware. Love is a beautiful bird, sent as messenger to my soul.

Chajala Pinu'u, healing Higher Power of I am I, I begin to understand the meaning of oneness and Sacred Law. Today and every day I have opportunities to think creatively and rely on my inner guide. I welcome the unfamiliar; I am glad for it! It moves me even closer to understanding Life's mysteries. Love is the salve of healing; when touched, it brings me rich and fulfilling knowledge.

Chajala Bidáá, healing Light of All That Is, learning has nourished my seed. I am in control of my attitude. Today is what I longed for. Light reveals the trees and the flowers to my eyes, and it brings love to my soul.

Reason and learning are functions of body and soul. Together they interact like the ever-changing winds. As the meaning of process soon comes to an end, the art of total being brings my ceremony to an end.

Daaiina. And so it is . . .

Horse Mountain Song

Maru'chii Nohwizá'yé, Spotted Runner of the Ancestors,
demonstrate the proper use of power, for on this day humanity
offers the power and the courage. For now humanity shines
forth upon the Changing Mother. As the Fourth World of
Separation departs Nakía announces the strength of the Fifth
World of Peace. I heed the true meaning of *warrior*. I have the
courage to challenge my fear. I come from the heart of the

Circle of Light to build upon my dreams the faith and hope of the new time. I come together with others to send forth upon the Changing Mother a new spirit with power to rise upon a foundation of peace. I come to praise mountains, to honor visions of those who have gone before. I come to dance my joy amidst the marvelous spirits of nature. I come to make my heart one with others, to make my soul an offering, to make my mind open to receiving.

Chajala Nakía, healing Snake of the South, surely you have prayed enough for this time to come, and henceforth you shall watch over the children of the Directions. For as you have come, separation departs. I have honored both times in truth. I move through fear to live in light, to love with passion.

Chajala Hada'didla, healing Thunderbeings of the Southwest, your showers of soft, warm rain nurture the seeds of dreams and create visions of magnitude. You are untethered purpose and pattern, breathing peace upon the land. My warrior's task is to embrace the change.

Chajala Eo'to'to, healing Bear of the West, guardian of the path of no judgement, the dream cave has provided the pure spring of the life of my community and I am like a drop of purity shimmering in the golden glow of Grandfather Sun. Facing the questions, searching, finding, committing—I am the Fifth World of Peace.

Chajala Dolee'atee, healing Little Ones of the Northwest, peace on the Changing Mother causes me to sing out the joy of the word, and I am alive to witness it. I am enveloped in the harmony of this world. Nothing is as important as this moment in time.

Chajala Tuma, healing Buffalo of the North, life I greet on this joyous occasion, while honor, health, and full respect I send forth into the galaxy to All My Relations. Opening myself, telling the truth about within—this is my Path of Beauty.

Chajala Kachiñas, healing Master Teachers of the Northeast, to smell a flower I call beauty, to hear its call, a gift from above. Who Spirit touches does live, who touches Spirit is free. To all the children, unconditional love I now give.

Chajala Itzá, healing Eagle of the East, justice lies in loving all. Justices lives within the truth. Justice soars upon wings of peace. Justice is here as peace and harmony prevail and new growth extends to all kin. As the children have taught, my actions now match my words.

Chajala Nohwizá'yé, healing Ancestors of the Southeast, when I love another I love myself in kind. When I give to another, true honor I have found. When I trust another, I embrace nobility. These are the Sacred Laws that live here. I no longer talk of peace. I feel the peace that is here.

Chajala Yusn, healing Giver of All Life, loving is a noble act. The living soul is such a beautiful sight. I meet love and recognize its law. To extend the heart with greater conviction brings pride that flies in Eagle's cry. Today I know peace.

Chajala Esonkñhsendehé, healing Changing Mother, the gifts of my new life spring from love's tear-filled eyes. Peace is the truth of my heart.

Chajala Echicasay, healing Higher Power of All My Relations, you are my kin, born of the same Mother. For even as I stand with you on this auspicious day I understand our oneness and know my true worth. I commit to peace. The shadow of fear I bring out, an entity no longer welcomed within.

Chajala Bidáá, healing Light of All That Is, the kindness of humanity is like a shell containing gem or precious pearl. With one heart do the people live; one deep softness. With integrity that is often revealed and compassion, too, the reward. Large, bright, an image so grand, humanity's soul now does come forth.

Empowering are the beliefs and teachings that make this day joyous. Truth is the goodness that leads me into celebration and sacredness, for it is my purpose to be happy upon Changing Mother and evolve into being all that I came here to be. I, who see love in this life, see fulfillment of ancient prophecy.

Daaiina. And so it is . . .

Owl Beauty in Darkness

Chawn Chissy, Grandfather Ghost Face, in this moment I am like the summit. I can see and hear others. And I am like the cave, birthing dreams and new visions of hope, prosperity, and love. I am the seed dropped by your hand into the field, breaking through my pod and waving my sapling leaves before the face of Grandfather Sun. I shall grow into a mighty tree, my roots in the heart of my sacred Mother,

Esonkñhsendehé, and my branches high in celebration of my
sacred Father, Yusn.

Chajala Nakía, healing Snake of the South, I am a devoted
child whispering into the ear of my inner self. I exercise my
power to act and feel the fullness of my being. Life is the
sacred incarnation of a smile.

Chajala Hada'didla, healing Thunderbeings of the Southwest,
I love to serve All My Relations with the faith of my love in
Spirit. I inform myself about who I am in my relationships.
Therein lies the solution to my problems.

Chajala Eo'to'to, healing Bear of the West, I am an oasis in
the desert, ready to quench the thirst of any seeker of the
heart. Stormy days freshen the air I breathe. Life is a spirit
who dwells in my soul, whose nourishment is borne of the
earth, and whose manifestation is the purpose of my being.

Chajala Dolee'atee, healing Little Ones of the Northwest,
peace is my duty and the Sacred Changing Mother the land
of my patriotism. Harmony is everywhere. I celebrate it. I
trust the present. I trust the future. Life that is lived in any
other manner is an illusion created from fear.

Chajala Tuma, healing Buffalo of the North, I have a yearning for my beautiful Relations. I do not turn my back on joy.
I am glad for all life's experiences. The panorama inspires me
fully. The spirits of Child of Water, Killer of Enemies, and
Snake Heart guide me through this time.

Chajala Kachiñas, healing Master Teachers of the Northeast, I love people because of their spirit. I celebrate our special and unique gifts today. My heart is lightened. The wealth of the world is within the eyes of our children.

Chajala Itzá, healing Eagle of the East, my relations rise, stimulated by their spirit to embrace the compassion of a new day. Every day, in every situation, I discover real joy. It's here. It accepted my invitation. Fear is a fog lying above the field. When Grandfather Sun mounts the horizon in his rays, joyful vision is revealed.

Chajala Nohwizá'yé, healing Ancestors of the Southeast, peace is on Earth, feeding the children and filling the stomachs of all with the great bounty of Esonkñhsendehé. I look at each moment with childish eyes. I find joy and contentment. Greatness lies in extending one's heart space without expectation.

Chajala Yusn, healing Giver of All Life, peace is here, within my heart. I enjoy the richness of today. My life weaves an intricate, necessary pattern that is uniquely mine. Unlimited love asks only for itself.

Chajala Esonkñhsendehé, healing Changing Mother, I laugh with the world and heal. I fear not failure or success. I experience neither alone; both are stepping stones on life's journey. This time in history calls for the nobility of the spirit, while dysfunction is disclosed for healing.

Chajala Pinu'u, healing Higher Power of I am I, I am peace. I appreciate the design of my life. I draw myself close to the moment. Laughter softens the feelings, and joy heals the heart.

Chajala Bidáá, healing Light of All That Is, peace is in the eyes of infants nursing on the breast of our great and sacred mother, Esonkñhsendehé. Negativity grows with attention. I nurture the positive. As laughter and joy are embraced the spirit of humanity will be like a completed tablet, inscribed with the signs of compassion and love.

I gaze upon the mountains and plains upon which Grandfather Sun throws his rays, and listen to the breeze singing the song of budding branches of spring, and inhale the fragrance of the flowers and honeysuckle, and say to myself, "What I see and hear are mine forever, and what I know and feel are my created reality." My humble soul sees and contemplates reverently the joys about me and embraces their existence: this is truth. I am a living soul celebrating my very existence, for I know all of Spirit's existing things.

Daaiina. And so it is . . .

Eagle's Rite of Coming Home

Itzá, Sacred White Tail, by nature I am unique and there is no limit that can apply to the full potential of my power. The truth of my untouched power has untold possibilities; today I leave the limitations of accomplished fact behind me. I hold onto the possibilities for good in what I believe.

Yusn and Esonkñhsendehé, the Sacred Parents, conspire to bring down peace for All My Relations.

Chajala Nakía, healing Snake of the South, from the beginning love is powerful. It changes the complexion of the universe. It changes the direction of my life. As a student of life I add each day to my stock of experience, knowing full well that the attainment of spirit is a different process.

Chajala Hada'didla, healing Thunderbeings of the Southwest, the possibility of repose makes All My Relations secure. We each have a friend whose flame flickers today. I help them and thus myself. A steady flame rekindles one that flickers. Each day I shed a self-centered impulse or desire and continue to do so until my will is at rest in Spirit and is undistracted.

Chajala Eo'to'to, healing Bear of the West, Yusn brings rebirth: I share our likeness and relish whatever differences surface. The chain of friendship I've created makes me the proud owner of wholeness. I am succeeding, moving forward with courage and self-awareness on this, my Path of Beauty. I let go of everything except All That Is; but having Spirit, I have the whole world with me.

Chajala Dolee'atee, healing Little Ones of the Northwest, who will object? Opportunities to react are many. I pause, determine the action I feel best about, and take it. My emotional healing gets a booster shot each time I make a responsible choice. The world is mine because I do not try to own it or control it according to my healing issues.

Chajala Tuma, healing Buffalo of the North, certainly I know the warrior's path asks me to view my intent in life. Are my relationships attachments, or are they based on love? I take inventory of them today. When I do not try to run things, then I win.

Chajala Kachiñas, healing Master Teachers of the Northeast, I have learned contentment. Combined we are one big orchestra. The conductor reads the music and directs the movements. Being in tune with the conductor feels good. I call it happiness. I play my part with joy. I have been advised that I can have everything I do not try to possess.

Chajala Itzá, healing Eagle of the East, I know my place in nature and I am secure in it. The miracles continue in my life. Everyday brings a miracle. Thankfulness helps me see the miracles at work in my life, and the lives of others, on the road to oneness. The closer I keep to the Changing Mother the more secure I feel in life.

Chajala Nohwizá'yé, healing Ancestors of the Southeast, I accept rebirth. I am never given more than I, and my higher power, can handle. I live within myself; I do not exhaust myself in fear's illusion.

Chajala Yusn, healing Giver of All Life, I belong to the eternal scheme of things. As I pass a friend I am grateful for her contribution to my wholeness. My perspicacity grows by small increments, but, by trusting in the light of Spirit, true wisdom comes to me.

Chajala Esonkñhsendehé, healing Changing Mother of All My Relations, all the strength I need is at hand. I let go and let Spirit help me. Everything depends on my relation to Spirit, especially the form of power appropriate to each interest and endeavor.

Chajala Pinu'u, healing Higher Power of I am I, it is only humanity that needs to learn wisdom. I listen to the music of today. I am in tune, in rhythm. I am part of the concert's beauty. This leads to the consideration of my true self, and actual purpose.

Chajala Bidáá, healing Light of All That Is, it is characteristic of Yusn that the truths I receive today guide my steps. I move in peace. My actualized self is the avenue through which my ideal self is contemplated.

Sacred Parents, you are everywhere, in everything, giving life to all. You are never coercive or possessive. You are of peaceful desire, and yet this is the measure of the greatness of All That Is. It is also the measure of greatness within myself as I conform to it.

Daaiina. And so it is . . .

nohwizá'yé bi kigoya'íi

Sharing
Ancestral
Wisdom

I do not know the true names for these matters of which I speak. We all have varying labels based on cultural appropriateness. Spirit always reveals itself in a manner that we are most comfortable with. What I do know is that our spirit flows through our veins, secretes in our organs, permeates our glands, and carries us on the breath of life. There is no part of a human being that is not engulfed by higher Spirit.

Even though our prayers address directional energies that play within the scope of our daily lives, we cannot speak in terms of within or without when we talk of the Spirit, for the Spirit is both: within and without. Spirit fills all space, all time, all dimensions. It is consciousness. It is not subjected to the limitations of our physical form but can range through all infinity, reaching to the height of our eventual evolution. It can travel the circumference of our world in a heartbeat. When we travel in our spirit flight to far-off places, where is our spirit?

The chore of the third spiral is to stop thinking in terms of measurements that permeate our lives and the physicality of our viewed reality. We have illusions to overcome, not obstacles. There is no space that is bounded by Spirit. Our consciousness can function in any dimension as our will dictates.

Labels are descriptions that help us comprehend in an intellectual manner. It is through experience without words, through felt concepts, that we shift in consciousness—that knowledge becomes an informed state of being. Spirit is within an expression of self. Spirit is without; it is our connection to the totality of all things. There is no knowledge in being that interprets Spirit apart from its expression, and as Spirit expresses itself, we come to know it. It is that part of ourselves that discerns between love and fear. It is the balance that enables us to understand that there is growth at all times. It is the purpose of our evolution.

Our essential body, our auric field, consists of the vibrations set up by the body. There are many layers, but the ones that are known to most are the auras that surround the physical body and the spiritual body. All things have auras—even rocks, plants, and animals have auras. All Our Relations contain and express life energy. The aura consists of the vibrations that emanate from the body and are organized according to the state of the body, so there are different vibrations. Those who can see the aura and can interpret it know the entire evolutional composite of the individual, if that person has given his permission for this viewing.

Health can be diagnosed in this manner. The state of the spirit and the mind's unfoldment in the creation of any dysfunctional situation or physical dis-ease is the key to healing. The history of evolution is availed, for it is this essence that enables us all to recognize one another in differing life patterns. Our auras register all that we have said, all that we have thought, and all that we have done. Our aura is our eternal history; there we can learn all that is contained within our hearts and the totality of all, the within and without.

The aura has to do with the healing of the Directions. All directions register in different colors.

The veil is thinning. The power of prayer is increasing. Manifestation is achieved through intense concentration, leaving an etheric picture that is registered in the minds of many along the threads of the web of life. This is what we have previously recognized as the "wrath of God" or a "blessed miracle."

The key to all of this is time. Time is not an illusion, but it has many dimensions. What is illusional is our measurement of time. Time itself is a reality. It exists. Space exists. But our measurements are not accurate because we view time and space from a limited focus. When we have the knowledge of other factors then the focus is more in flow with the energies of the universe.

We register on our auras every deed, every thought, every word so that we are the result of our own evolution, known to all those who have gone before and will come again. Being responsible in deed or word or thought, our own evolution succeeds as a result.

There is no integrity unless there is always integrity. There is a time for silence. This leads to the moment when truth is known.

Nothing—no physical or psychological or educational or cultural or religious thought—can affect the evolution of our soul. We are only affected by the expression of thought and intent in our daily lives. We reconcile the difference between our soul's evolution and our limited expression through physicality.

We awaken. The time is now.

There is an attraction. We create our own reality. It is time to live our lives in conditions of harmony, responsibly co-creating, in connection with All Our Relations. Reality evolves.

All Our Relations are alive, responding to vibrations that we may still not understand. The Ancients have left ways to use these vibrations and once again open the lines of communication.

When we withdraw from this life the work of this path shifts; then we return for the next leg of our journey. When, in the next earthwalk, we withdraw and return, we resolve ourselves once more into the elements of which we have called ourselves into being. For as we are one with Spirit, we are always one with Spirit.

Everything in the universe vibrates, and vibrations from all things are constantly being radiated along the threads of the web of life. All vibrations send out rays and all these rays carry influence. A beginning knowledge of all vibrations helps, for there is a Sacred Law, a tidbit of guidance behind them all.

There are millions of ways of expressing truth because truth is of the Sacred Parents, and it can be expressed according to the evolution of the individual through whom it is being expressed. It is through simplicity that we learn truth. We release the veil of forgetfulness as we set about on our journey into remembrance.

Crow's Original Memory

Angwusna, Grandmother Crow, you bring the breath of life.
You gave us liberty. You, who light our way with Spirit's fire,
kindle the flame that burns within my soul.

Ukehé Nakía, I am grateful Snake of the South. I sit by my fire
and watch the smoke rise to join the essence of all inspiration.
Combined, we are one big orchestra. The conductor reads the
music and directs movements. Being in tune with the conduc-

tor feels good. I call it happiness. I play my part with joy. I am now as one of the Ancients.

Ukehé Hada'didla, I am grateful Thunderbeings of the Southwest. I have hope. I take action in every lesson engaging me—I turn to Spirit. Each lesson is an invitation to inner peace. The Ancients and I are one.

Ukehé Eo'to'to, I am grateful Bear of the West. I release all despair that is past; my dreams today guide me. I take my first step into this Dream Reality. Thus I speak as one who measures the world's conscience by Spirit's vision.

Ukehé Dolee'atee, I am grateful Little Ones of the Northwest. I find All My Relations united and enjoying one great faith. Restlessness is a barometer that reveals my spiritual health. Prayer is called for today. I measure the range of all existence by the infinite lineage of creation.

Ukehé Tuma, I am grateful Buffalo of the North. I abound in love. Every day is a training ground. Every experience trains me to recognize the value of succeeding experiences. With richness I develop, one moment at a time. Grandfather Sun warms me in his gentle embrace, and the sea washes my soul with the foam of manifestation.

Ukehé Kachiñas, I am grateful Master Teachers of the Northeast. My soul is a well-tilled field. I live in the present. I choose to. Gentle reminders are sometimes necessary. I step into my life today. It is a habit I never want to break. My heart space keeps Spirit's love secret no more. My inner child no longer hides from those we see, and we, together, have clarity.

Ukehé Itzá, I am grateful Eagle of the East. My passion is stoked by Spirit's desire; living life is much more than just being alive. I choose to jump in with both feet. Wisdom awaits me in the depths. I reveal secrets and I am considered courageous; silence and secrecy cannot exist in a heart filled with love.

Ukehé Nohwizá'yé, I am grateful Ancestors of the Southeast. I have found peace; a deep breath invites the inner strength to move through me. I feel the exhilaration of Spirit's power. I know the excitement of growth and peace. The seed that the pine cone contains in its heart is the secret of the Tree of Peace, from the beginning of all creation.

Ukehé Yusn, I am grateful Giver of All Life. I see my truth within the fire. The mixture of calm with storm is not haphazard. Quite the contrary, growth is at the center of each. Spirit knows no segregation among words or names. Spirit doesn't label, judge, or compartmentalize. Spirit blesses all the same. I am grateful for this dynamic of life.

Ukehé Esonkñhsendehé, I am grateful Changing Mother. I am reborn. I enjoy the richness of today. My life weaves an intricate, necessary pattern that is uniquely mine. I am empowered by Spirit to pray and envision fervently, until that for which I am projecting begins far from my eyes, whereupon my higher self opens the way.

Ukehé Pinu'u, I am grateful Higher Power of I am I.
I worship Spirit. The truths I receive today guide my steps.
I move in peace. I see my higher self, and in doing so I see
the truth of sacred purpose for myself, for All My Relations,
for All That Is.

Ukehé Bidáá, I am grateful Light of All That Is. This time is
a phase of evolution in our daily growth; I relish the joy at
hand. I share my wisdom. All painful pasts brighten someone's future when openly shared. The standing mutely by is
a vain stance of a nonexistent reality. In possessing what I
have within myself, I have become who I am now.

All My Relations, I am faithful and find the goodness of
you the foundation for the Fifth World of Peace, in whose
souls the essence of perfection touches Spirit. You are the lilies
in the garden of truth. It is your fragrance that I breathe in for
strength and disperse upon the ethers of universal family,
where it will eternally regenerate the life force of creation.
Daaiina. And so it is . . .

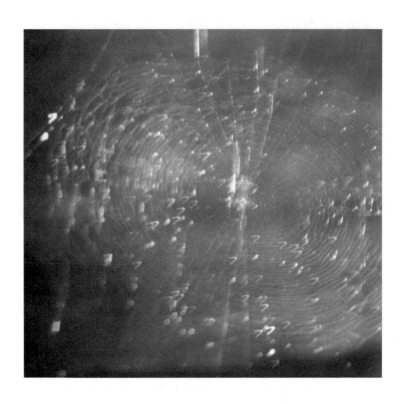

Otter's Gathering
of Spirit

Skuk'ach Nan, Grandmother Otter, play and miracles are the norm for life, for you have promised them. The power and ways have been given to us to be passed on to others. I keep them and get more by giving them away. I pray and leave my offering in gratitude, knowing that the answer is on its way to me. I constantly look for it as I go about my daily tasks.

Ukehé Nakía, I am grateful Snake of the South. I accept what happens and bathe in the wonder of it. There is no need to struggle. I breathe deeply and travel with my higher power wherever it takes me. The doors are open for as far as I can see. This does not take away my regular responsibilities.

Ukehé Hada'didla, I am grateful Thunderbeings of the Southwest. I do not waste time on the why's and wherefore's. Life offers chances to be wildly enthusiastic and chances to be deadly serious. I focus on the middle ground and cultivate my sense of honor. I continue to share in the work that has to be done at home, making my contributions to the needs of my community.

Ukehé Eo'to'to, I am grateful Bear of the West. The Sacred Parents have given me a magnificent mind and natural power that I am expected to use—intimacy lets me help another also live a full and peace-filled life. I reach out to someone today. In fact, I do what I do for my community and All My Relations.

Ukehé Dolee'atee, I am grateful Little Ones of the Northwest. I recognize that putting myself completely in Spirit's infinitely capable hands is for my own best good. Each and every expression of love I offer makes smooth another step I take in life. I am called to be a clean conduit for my circle and for anyone else I can help. I do not seek power for personal use and honor.

Ukehé Tuma, I am grateful Buffalo of the North. My fervent wish is to share the Sacred Parents' gifts with as many as I can reach. I look around me today and I am thankful. I tell someone close that I am glad we share one another's world. I become the pipeline that connects Spirit, All My Relations, and the universal consciousness, united.

Ukehé Kachiñas, I am grateful Master Teachers of the Northeast. We need more of the human community coming into circle, sharing prayers and celebrating life. I help others face anguish. It brings us together. It softens me. It makes way for laughter. This tells me the direction my curing and healing work must follow and establishes the kind of life I must lead.

Ukehé Itzá, I am grateful Eagle of the East. I take the transference of power seriously. As I pass a friend I am grateful for his contribution to my wholeness. I am strong and committed and stick with my path.

Ukehé Nohwizá'yé, I am grateful Ancestors of the Southeast. I ask you to rid me of everything about me that will impede me in any way, such as doubt, questions, or reluctance. Stormy days freshen the air I breathe. The lessons I am taught by my human teachers stress that the healing of self is important in terms of what this teaches the entire community.

Ukehé Yusn, I am grateful Giver of All Life Above. I recognize myself as a clean conduit ready to be filled with hope and possibilities and anxious to be filled with power; each step taken is in harmony with my higher power. I experience nothing alone. I breathe in and tap the plentiful source of strength, the eternal Now. The community must continue to know that Spirit and All Our Relations are always with it, and that it need not be afraid.

Ukehé Esonkñhsendehé, I am grateful Changing Mother Below. I experience the power as it comes surging into me; I make my day. I project the flavor of today's experiences. I lift my spirits and know all is well. Seeing a person healed gives the community assurance that we are not alone, and it gives strength to carry on.

Ukehé Pinu'u, I am grateful Higher Power of I am I. I give the power away to others in the knowledge that, as I am emptied out, the Sacred Parents will keep filling me with even greater power to be given away. Emotional health depends on active involvement in deciding who I am right now. Deciding to chuckle rather than snarl gives me an emotional boost. I sit in the center of every important thing that goes on in my community and in the web of life, and when power is set in motion it brings us more in contact with the totality of All That Is.

Ukehé Bidáá, I am grateful Light of All That Is. As I close my eyes I have the distinct sensation that Itzá, Eagle, is hovering close around me. I hear just what I need to hear today. I open myself fully to the words. I emphasize that prevention is more important than treatment where the community and individuals are concerned.

I hear the shrill cry of Eagle. I face the east and kneel. I close my eyes and breathe deeply seven times to begin my immersion into the spirit of this time. When I am done, I rest and listen for Spirit's response.

Daaiina. And so it is . . .

Roadrunner's Ancient Way

Quo-Qui, Swift Windrunner, if anything puzzles me about life it is my inability to understand why others do not see the Path of Beauty and walk the way of inner peace. I aim for the Star Nations and project visions that once seemed beyond reach. I have enjoyed the challenges this has brought. I learned how to not be perfect.

Ukehé Nakía, I am grateful Snake of the South. Today I am in my truth. I know Spirit's will when I listen to my inner voice. I do what feels responsible, and peace is always my reward. I co-create with higher powers.

Ukehé Hada'didla, I am grateful Thunderbeings of the Southwest. All experiences make a positive contribution to my being. My time has come. I co-create my future. I take each day, each experience, as it draws me to the next important step. Others seek me out because they are curious and want to know why my life works.

Ukehé Eo'to'to, I am grateful Bear of the West. I am humbled by the magnificence of my life. I let my healing shine its light in my life. My monsters flee. The greatest miracle is not something incredible—it's the thousands of little things that change lives.

Ukehé Dolee'atee, I am grateful Little Ones of the Northwest. I exercise my power as it and I again become one. Harmony is everywhere. I celebrate it. I trust the present. I trust the future. Miracles are created by believers.

Ukehé Tuma, I am grateful Buffalo of the North. Things are seldom automatic in relationships. I strengthen my supports, my connection to others, for the success of each of us. I express my love and assure my loved ones that they are needed. We surge ahead with new life. I wish to be authentic, so I am a person of faith, and I can only live in harmony if my faith is involved in every area of my life.

Ukehé Kachiñas, I am grateful Master Teachers of the North-east. I learn from you what I am made of so I can experience things more fully. All events, all experiences, are connected. The path I travel, alone and with others, brings me brighter days. I trust my path. It's right for me. Good intentions are only the beginning. My guides and I are glued together in faith for the healing to occur.

Ukehé Itzá, I am grateful Eagle of the East. I step aside to care for myself when I must, knowing always to return to the Source. What a wonderful collection of invitations I have! I live my life in beauty!

Ukehé Nohwizá'yé, I am grateful Ancestors of the Southeast. Your presence gives me confidence and gets me ready for the future adventure. I relish the joy at hand. I share my wisdom. All painful pasts brighten someone's future when openly shared. As long as I have the strength to do Spirit's will, I am faithful constantly.

Ukehé Yusn, I am grateful Giver of All Life. I exercise my healing power on the little things—on small wounds and situations that are irritants, avoidable precursors to imbalance. I pay particular attention to the accomplishments of others—those close to me and those I read or hear about. I believe their example and feel the forward push. Although I keep my life in balance, I don't waste my time.

Ukehé Esonkñhsendehé, I am grateful Changing Mother. While the power comes into and through me, it does not change the fact that I am of human form. I strengthen my supports, my connection to others, for the success of each of us. I express my love and assure my loved ones that they are needed. We surge ahead with new life. We can do anything if we focus our intent.

Ukehé Pinu'u, I am grateful Higher Power of I am I. The higher powers work with me as I am; I am more receptive with experience. My love of another is a contributing factor in that person's growth. The loving gratitude of another enhances my own endeavors. I take a moment with a friend who needs my love. I take the time to experience things to know how they truly are.

Ukehé Bidáá, I am grateful Light of All That Is. As I close my eyes to become a clean conduit of Spirit's energy of unconditional love, I live as if I have done this already. I begin to do it. The lessons of love increase my rapture. Can we know how rain or snow feels without being out in it?

I love All My Relations. They are my first thought. I am a person of high integrity. I am responsible in my co-creations. I am a good friend.

Daaiina. And so it is . . .

Snake Children
Fire of Healing

Nakía, Snake of Sky Eyes, in the silence I open myself to
Sacred Law and universal order, calmly seeking guidance. I
am a powerful entity knowing my own strength, confident in
my existence and a believer in my destiny.

Ukehé Nakía, I am grateful Snake of the South. In this cycle I
repeat the lessons I do not understand. My effort is successful.

Opportunities to share my secrets present themselves today. I am courageous. My heart hears more than the notes in the song of the nightingale.

Ukehé Hada'didla, I am grateful Thunderbeings of the Southwest. This time is between sleeping and waking. My attitude makes this day what it becomes. Meeting it head on with love assures me of a lovely day. My heart hears my ant friends as they speak within their subterranean labyrinth, urging me to be patient. I am.

Ukehé Eo'to'to, I am grateful Bear of the West. I hold the soil of the past and the seeds of the future within my hands. We each have a friend whose flame flickers today. I help my friend and thus myself. A steady flame rekindles one that flickers. Nature reaches out to me with welcoming arms and bids me enjoy her beauty. I embrace her silence and rush into her caress, there to nurture and grow strong with my cousin the Snake.

Ukehé Dolee'atee, I am grateful Little Ones of the Northwest. Oh spirits of childhood dreams, life offers me a chance for greater happiness today. I'm growing! To Nature all are alive and all are free.

Ukehé Tuma, I am grateful Buffalo of the North. You who watches over me from the great medicine bowl of eternity. It feels good to help others feel appreciated. Love and acceptance is my lifeline from Spirit encircling us all. The earthly glory of humanity is a fulfilling prophecy, manifesting with the bubbles in the rocky stream.

Ukehé Kachiñas, I am grateful Master Teachers of the Northeast. I go to the altar you have adorned with the pearls of your thoughts and the gems of your souls because I am free of oppression now and always. I discover my creativity. It's here. I have released it from the clutches of my ego. I heard the brook humming as a mother to her child and I sang joyfully, "Life is pure and good."

Ukehé Itzá, I am grateful Eagle of the East. My prayers are as light as the clouds and as peaceful as the breeze. I behave the way I decide to. I choose to think about others and love them. I choose to forget about myself. I am compelled to go to All My Relations and embrace them and offer them a sweeter drink and assist them in their search for truth, sharing my purity and turning my goodness free upon the ethers of the universe.

Ukehé Nohwizá'yé, I am grateful Ancestors of the Southeast. You, the real beacons of light on my path, bless me. In the moment lives spirit within. In the moment I am creative, blessed with gifts like no other. I stay in the moment and offer those gifts, guided by Spirit's will. I heard the birds chanting, and I joined in: "Beauty is the law of all times."

Ukehé Yusn, I am grateful Giver of All Life. I belong in this time. I find happiness. Searching within myself I patiently, trustingly, share myself with others. A bird flew near and perched at the tip of a branch and said, "Child of the Sacred Parents, come into the field and celebrate life with us as your relations."

Ukehé Esonkñhsendehé, I am grateful Changing Mother. My prayers are answered today; my time has come. I co-create my future. I take each day, each experience—they draw me to the next important step. We are now joining together, for we know we are *go-tah*, we are family.

Ukehé Pinu'u, I am grateful I am I. I am a breath of immortality. I fine-tune my value system today. Every experience is an opportunity to express that definition. Now Grandfather Sun rises from behind the mountain peaks and gilds the treetops with coronals.

Ukehé Bidáá, I am grateful Light of All That Is. You have made me wiser. I make the right choices. I know what they are because I ask for guidance. I look upon this beauty and say to myself *Pinu' Echicasay*, I am All My Relations.

Yesterday is happily released; today, joyfully embraced. I walk in light. I walk with my eyes focused on Grandfather Sun. I am beautiful in my knowing, virtuous in my ways, and strong in my faith. Today I am ingenious, sincere, and full of heart in my knowledge. Beauty and knowledge, ingenuity and virtue, strength of body and spirit are united within me on this day.

Daaiina. And so it is . . .

Frog's Victory Dance

Swalah'kin, Green Rainmaker, the Sacred Parents have given all things life. This includes the stone people, standing tall ones, water, and the ground I walk upon. And just as the two-legged, four-legged, winged, creepy crawlies, and those that swim in the sea have blood in them, so too everything else has thoughts, feelings, concerns, and hopes.

Ukehé Nakía, I am grateful Snake of the South. I talk to you like I talk to another person, and I let you talk to me. I exercise my prayers because I want the spiritual security where I find joy. I ask for guidance with every experience today. Nakía, do what you do naturally.

Ukehé Hada'didla, I am grateful Thunderbeings of the Southwest. You tell me where you have come from, what you have seen, what you have heard, and what you feel. My time has come. I co-create my future. I take each day, each experience. They draw me to the next important step. I revere all things. Human life itself depends on how we treat other life.

Ukehé Eo'to'to, I am grateful Bear of the West. We are friends. I am never given more than I, and my Higher Power, can handle. My reverence is for the whole of creation, both the animate and the inanimate.

Ukehé Dolee'atee, I am grateful Little Ones of the Northwest. When we are finished this day I have a whole new picture of you. Every day is a training ground. Every experience trains me to recognize the value of future experiences. With richness I develop, one moment at a time. With Spirit, everything is possible.

Ukehé Tuma, I am grateful Buffalo of the North. Doing this expands the way I behave toward other things, and my mind grows. I take a look at where I am today. I am grateful for who I am. It's right for me now and prepares me for the adventure at hand. The adventure begins with self-healing.

Ukehé Kachiñas, I am grateful Master Teachers of the Northeast. The more I do "becoming," the wiser I become about everything. Full attention to the persons sent to me

offers me exactly what I need. My higher self beckoned them.
I am alert; I expect healing and celebrate the wonder of it all.
I let Spirit and the guides of the Directions heal me so I
know how healing works.

Ukehé Itzá, I am grateful Eagle of the East. I carry the practice of "becoming" even further. I move forward; we all move
forward. I am on target. I participate in a glorious, wonderful
play. I jump for joy. I am specially blessed. Now this understanding can be sent out from me to the rest of creation.

Ukehé Nohwizá'yé, I am grateful Ancestors of the Southeast.
Whenever I am making a ritual I pick up an item that represents you and press it to my chest. Prayer and meditation
direct my efforts. My purpose is fulfilled. I can be a clean
conduit for healing the world, just as I can be a conduit for
curing, healing, and helping others.

Ukehé Yusn, I am grateful Giver of All Life. I am becoming
you and identifying with you in order to experience you and
understand you completely. In this day that stands before me
I am certain that I have many chances for growth, for kindness to others, for developing my own confidence. I am
thoughtful in my actions; they are special and will be
repeated no more. All That Is created the Sacred Parents so
that we will do everything to take care of All Our Relations.

Ukehé Esonkñhsendehé, I am grateful Changing Mother.
Beyond the obvious implications of the gesture, what excites
me is knowing that establishing such a relationship to All
That Is is the core principle of healing. I take action even

when I'm afraid. Action produces growth, and without growth there is no life. I live! Everything fulfills its role—ants, worms, vultures, wolves, pebbles, sand—everything. I care for these and for you, Changing Mother, as I care for myself.

Ukehé Pinu'u, I am grateful I am I. As I press different power items to my body I identify with the powers they represent and I am given a heightened sense of life and longevity that attend the supernatural world. I look around me at others, and I remember that my growth and theirs depends on loving and being loved. I reach out. I make love new. Everything in creation is alive, makes its particular contribution, and has special value.

Ukehé Bidáá, I am grateful Light of All That Is. Because I believe your life force is fed to me when I walk in balance, it has a profound effect upon my self-healing system. I carefully look about me today with gladness at the teachers I've selected to learn from. I am only one part of a giant web whose assemblage of strands, working cooperatively together, accounts for its overall strength.

Everything that has been created is essential to life and balance and harmony. Everything has feelings. This is how I think and how I define life. I believe something has life, so it has life. Spirit taught me to think about creation this way; when I do, the life all things have within becomes apparent to me, and I treat those beings accordingly. I do not abuse or misuse them. When I pray each day I pray for the health and healing of the whole of creation, not just for humanity's healing. And I ask Spirit and the guides of the Directions to help me walk on Changing Mother with compassion and understanding for all that exists.

Daaiina. And so it is . . .

Butterfly's Celebration of Children

I remember you, *Ichi'kíí*, Flower Maiden, living here. Our relations make me smile, contributing to a wonderful day. As is so often the case, they simply are, and so are part of me. You make me cry and shout for joy, all within this moment in time.

Ukehé Nakía, I am grateful Snake of the South. My gratitude plays an important role in my visioning. Full attention to those sent to me offers me exactly what I need. My higher self beckoned them. I am alert; I expect healing and celebrate the wonder of it all. It can be seen that through visioning, without having learned the biological manner in which the left and right brain work, I am taught a lifeway that draws naturally on the right brain.

Ukehé Hada'didla, I am grateful Thunderbeings of the Southwest. When I vision with my mind, eyes, and heart I see through the eyes of the Higher Powers, without limitations. I have no fears today. Nothing I can't handle, in fact, nothing I can't grow from comes my way. My inner strength sees me through. Visioning is like opening a door, but I must walk through the door to experience the wondrous things that are in the great and magical room on the other side.

Ukehé Eo'to'to, I am grateful Bear of the West. Aside from the usual things a nose does, like breathing, it stirs up my memories, so it works like a treasure chest that connects me to the joyful experiences of the past. Today's issues deserve a fresh response. I am not afraid. Today flows from yesterday, the day before, and the day before that. Tomorrow will follow suit, and when I get there it is absolutely fundamental that I "believe in order to see," rather than follow the scientific approach of seeing in order to believe.

Ukehé Dolee'atee, I am grateful Little Ones of the Northwest. Smells are associated with everything we do. I will think of you each time I smell (*Reader: insert your own thought*), and I shall smile. Secrets promote dis-ease. I listen, I share, and I am well. How else can Spirit and the guides of the Directions show their wonders to me?

Ukehé Tuma, I am grateful Buffalo of the North. The Giver of All Life has covered Changing Mother with All My Relations, and we combine our efforts to produce peace. Emotional health depends on active involvement in deciding who I am right now. Deciding to chuckle rather than snarl gives me an emotional boost. The mouth is what we taste with, eat with, and communicate with. But it is also what gets us into trouble!

Ukehé Kachiñas, I am grateful Master Teachers of the Northeast. Our sweet plant relations, like sweetgrass and sage, love me and turn fear away, since its only connection is negative illusion. Every day is a gift-giving time because I make it so. In my initial quest for vision I was given certain powerful medicine and numerous ways to perform healing rites. All I need do is remember.

Ukehé Itzá, I am grateful Eagle of the East. I wear sage in the *diyi'ni hedowachee*, the holyway festivals of joy, to draw the Higher Powers close because they recognize sage as honoring the sacredness in life. I teach myself reverence. I begin today. I look for Spirit everywhere, and I find it. Spirit has given me powerful healing songs and three of the most phenomenal meditation and focusing tools ever handed down to humankind. I consider today what these might be.

Ukehé Nohwizá'yé, I am grateful Ancestors, you who urge me to feel, to want, and to create. Today I pay particular attention to the accomplishments of others—those close to me and those I read or hear about. I believe in their example and feel the forward push. Along with my joining with others in *diyi'ni hedowachee*, purification, and entering the silence, my diligent employment of songs and tools plays a great role in connecting and partnering with the power that Spirit and the guides of the Directions add to my own.

Ukehé Yusn, I am grateful Giver of All Life, you who provides an atmosphere of mystery and ancient wisdom and stirs my inner calling. Today's dreams and experiences are signs on the path of my life. I do not pass them without notice. One tool enables me to do thought transference—conveying thoughts and images to other people, assisting them in their healing, and allowing them to help me in mine.

Ukehé Esonkñhsendehé, I am grateful Changing Mother. Everything that exists has an essence, and when we pass close by one another there is a bond of love between us. My time has come. I co-create my future. I take each day, each experience. They draw me to the next important step. A second tool empowers me with continual strength, longevity, and regeneration by giving me a wondrous way to achieve daily rebirth, renewal, fertility, and thanksgiving.

Ukehé Echicasay, I am grateful All My Relations. This is how *go-tah*, family, comes into being. I take care of my inner child today. Together we face the adventure of life. The third tool is a stunning sacred prayer-feather offering, whose use allows me to continually offer my entire self for service to the Higher Powers.

Ukehé Bidáá, I am grateful Light of All That Is. Esonkñhsendehé, Changing Mother, and the guides of the Directions use love to communicate with me—sometimes in words, but more often to stir up my mind and heart to think of spiritual things. This morning is blessing number one! It is important for me to acknowledge that I believe everyone can use the same tools I possess to accomplish everything I do.

Esonkñhsendehé, Changing Mother, you speak to me through the drum. Rattles are the soft voice of Yusn, the Giver of All Life, sending showers of blessings upon this world. Flutes are the voices of the *naadin di'i'i*, the guides of the Directions. *Ta-tonka*, Old Man Thunder, is the powerful voice of the awesome Thunderbeings. It is the ears that rocks speak to first, and through the ears to the mind, spirit, and heart. All Our Relations that exist or are coming into being are the Sacred Parents' children; like the other beautiful children they have had, they love me. They come closer when I honor them. I know they are there and sharing every experience with me.

Daaiina. And so it is . . .

Celebrating Turtle Island

Ya-wé, Grandmother Turtle, it is always the same where embracing our sacredness is concerned. We learn, purify with smoke, and work in service to the whole of creation. All takes time, and during this time we enter deeper and deeper into communion with Yusn, the Giver of All Life, and *naadin di'i'i*, the guides of the Directions. This gives them the time they need to work in and through us, and together we accomplish magnificent things. This is a time of going more intensely into the energy. We feel it more and we think about it more. In this ceremony our daily life and any distractions have been put aside, and we are ready to receive the power of co-creation and set it in motion.

Ukehé Nakía, I am grateful Snake of the South. I rise slowly to my feet and stretch my arms and legs. I look around me and I am thankful. I tell someone close that I am glad we share one another's world. When we are together transformation experiences occur. I can always turn some part of the projected dream or vision into tangible reality.

Ukehé Hada'didla, I am grateful Thunderbeings of the Southwest. I stir the coals of my eternal flame and feed the fire within. I am still and commune with Spirit. I am patient, humble, and peaceful through love. If, for example, feathers appear to me, I can catch several of them out of the air. They are blessings of peace from my winged relations.

Ukehé Eo'to'to, I am grateful Bear of the West. Sparks swarm into the air like busy bees in service to community, and the rich fragrance of sage floats through my memory. My relationships with others are as healthy and fulfilling as my communication with Spirit. On this occasion, as I am with you, you move the energy and leave something warm and glowing within my being.

Ukehé Dolee'atee, I am grateful Little Ones of the Northwest. I close my eyes and inhale deeply. Depression must be coddled to maintain it. I chose a long time ago to move beyond depression. Now I help others banish it from their lives. I enjoy the results. My ability to do this comes through people's stories, which are built upon the foundation of experiential truth. The stories are true to the individuals and are never dismissed.

Ukehé Tuma, I am grateful Buffalo of the North. Purple-ash butte, red mahogany, yellow pine, and thick grass is a sublime place to be—sacred space. A deep breath invites the inner strength to move through me. I feel the exhilaration of Spirit's power. I know the excitement of growth and peace. I believe that the path I walk has taken shape over a long period of time—in fact, the unblemished core has always remained, and I have never been alone in charting my course.

Ukehé Kachiñas, I am grateful Master Teachers of the Northeast. To go with you is to walk back into sacred history—the Ancestors are there. The miracles continue in my life. Every day brings a miracle. Thankfulness helps me see the miracles at work in my life, and the lives of others, on the road to oneness. There are legends from the Ancestors that explain the existence and way of things.

Ukehé Itzá, I am grateful Eagle of the East. This particular day I notice the colors black, turquoise, yellow, and white. Many opportunities to make choices present themselves. The choices I make satisfy me; they move me toward my goal of wholeness. There is a big difference between a healing story and a victim's story.

Ukehé Nohwizá'yé, I am grateful Ancestors of the Southeast. I adjust my energy so that it is centered and begin to sing a song that has a pleasing melody. It feels good to help others feel appreciated. Love and acceptance is my lifeline from Spirit, encircling us all. Old-paradigm patterns keep telling us how things are, but in my lifetime one illusion has been revealed, giving way to another, in a process that has forced fear to keep reinventing itself and its strategy. The prophecies are playing out. Peace is at hand.

Ukehé Yusn, I am grateful Giver of All Life. I catch a few words I recognize about how blessed we are to know Spirit. Today stretches forth, an unknown quantity. Concerns crowd, but guidance regarding the best action to take is always available. When I go within I find evidence that supports the truth of origin.

Ukehé Esonkñhsendehé, I am grateful Changing Mother. Purification has ended. We integrate for a moment. We know that there are always songs in our hearts when we live life responsibly because we are so happy. I step toward today with assurance, reaching out to others along the way, trusting that my accumulated steps add stability to my future. It is that way with transformation.

Ukehé Pinu'u, I am grateful I am I. Regarding transformation and thought transference, there have been numerous instances where the Higher Powers have worked phenomenal things in and through me. I am not weary, disillusioned, or disappointed. My trust is in the way of Spirit. When I am transformed and projecting my intent, the person or the group sees what I am seeing, and also what is happening to me.

Ukehé Bidáá, I am grateful Light of All That Is. Among my experiences there were some through which I was transformed and some through which—despite the unusual things that occurred—I was not. Decisions are called for today. I am patient with myself, and thoughtful. I listen closely to the guidance that comes from those around me. The message that comes to me when I am transformed is not completely different from the messages I receive when I am projecting intent.

We use white clouds to pull our intent together as one. We tie *paho*, prayer feathers, as offerings of gratitude to the trees and bushes here on the sacred land. We keep the memory of this time to assist us so shadow may never fall.

Daaiina. And so it is . . .

Festival of the Dead

Nohwiẓá'yé, Ancestors, you who have gone before. While others may only do personal ceremony as occasional events, through these prayer wheels and my daily time in silence Spirit has given me a way to continuously experience the powerful benefits of affirming my connection. For me, this personal ceremony has become an ongoing fountain of energy, transference, expansion, peace, fertility, and transcendence that I can call upon whenever I need to.

Ukehé Nakía, I am grateful Snake of the South. I was given this renewal tool as vision, as I rise to my feet and bounce around to loosen the energy, and I use it. I celebrate our special and unique gifts today. My heart is lightened. Whenever I do ceremony of this nature I receive the messages I need to receive for a period of four days.

Ukehé Hada'didla, I am grateful Thunderbeings of the Southwest. I have been given the vitality to keep doing things as the *naadin di'i'i,* the guides of the Directions, work in and through me. I flow with the energetic tide. It assuredly moves me closer to my destination. This is how I tell the *naadin di'i'i* that I really appreciate what they have done for me.

Ukehé Eo'to'to, I am grateful Bear of the West. The work of a holy person is never ending. I look for my lessons and feel exhilarated by the growth guaranteed. The *naadin di'i'i,* the guides of the Directions, send extra blessings to me for this.

Ukehé Dolee'atee, I am grateful Little Ones of the Northwest. I am to use this connection for myself during my lifetime, and as I pass through this life I pass it on to others. I realize that Spirit provides everything I need. I know that Spirit's power is always available. I am a resplendent being of creation.

Ukehé Tuma, I am grateful Buffalo of the North. I am assured the world is interested in all this, as it comes from Spirit. I am not about to argue with that. Many opportunities to make choices present themselves. The choices I make satisfy me; they move me toward my goal of wholeness. I go into nature and pray.

Ukehé Kachiñas, I am grateful Master Teachers of the Northeast. I am overflowing with energy, smiling and ready to go. As I come together with friends and family I listen for Spirit's message. I hear what I need to hear because I listen. When I come to Spirit I hold the knowledge I receive with the greatest care, my eyes misting. A soft smile demonstrates to all how much I cherish and respect what Spirit brings to me.

Ukehé Itzá, I am grateful Eagle of the East. Regeneration takes approximately an hour, and because I spend time in this communion I accomplish a great deal more than I otherwise could have. I rest from my thoughts. I give my attention wholly to the present. Therein comes the solution, when least expected. I smell sweet tobacco smoke and sweetgrass and I am impregnated with the spirit of Itzá, the Eagle.

Ukehé Nohwizá'yé, I am grateful Ancestors of the Southeast. Now I do it. The forgiving heart is magical. My whole life undergoes a dynamic change when I develop a forgiving heart. I made the choice to walk this path many years ago. I have no regrets, only great joy in my choice.

Ukehé Yusn, I am grateful Giver of All Life. I hold out my hands to receive the gifts you bring. I chose healing. I said, "I can help it." I celebrate that I take responsibility for my life today. I want you, Giver of All Life, and the Sacred Changing Mother, to know that I am here to serve you.

Ukehé Esonkñhsendehé, I am grateful Changing Mother. I am beaming and feel very good. When I am uncomfortable with certain situations, and the feelings don't leave, I consider what might transmute the energy. I open myself to the way and ask to be shown the steps necessary. This day represents me and my thoughts, along with my love and devotion to the *naadin di'i'i*, the guides of the Directions.

Ukehé Pinu'u, I am grateful I am I. I can feel the energy and enthusiasm radiating from my being. Peace is here. I look to Spirit, and only to Spirit, and know all is well. I am all that I need to be. I express my continuing gratitude for what the *naadin di'i'i* have done in and through me for myself and others.

Ukehé Bidáá, I am grateful Light of All That Is. I shrug my shoulders, release, and hold out my hands. The forgiving heart is magical. My whole life undergoes dynamic change each time I release with a forgiving heart. In appearance, I am a fabulous creation.

I do my renewal time of silence. Then, following closely as I can what I am told, I walk in the footsteps of *nohwizá'yé*, the Ancestors. I sing my gratitude for all that is forthcoming and feel absolutely superb and fully regenerated. It is as if the weight of the previous day has never existed. It has rolled away, and my creative thoughts are racing ahead.

　Daaiina. And so it is . . .

nohwizá'yé bizhíí

Speaking with the Ancestor's Voice

We are now learning how to serve. This work was created to teach, through service, that we can influence our world by the power of thought. Much can be accomplished by intensive thought of those who desire to uplift humanity. We learn concentration to enable us to help birth a new world—a world of peace—guided by Sacred Law. Our spiritual guides are a source of strength to us, because they have joined with us in partnership to help us through this evolutional process.

There is no separation, because all dimensions are part of All That Is. We are awakening to this fact. We cannot ignore it. And who would really want to?

Nothing is lost in this time. As we express ourselves we unfold and evolve. The higher we evolve, the more we realize that we must express ourselves. So we always seek to further our evolution by finding a way through which our personal medicine powers—our talents—can be revealed. Sometimes that inspiration is unconscious; sometimes it is known. Sometimes so strong is the impressing urge for expression that the true identity of our spiritual self is revealed in the inspiration.

Inspiration is collective and individual, because all energy that exists is in cooperation. All energy that we expend is in group service, whether we are aware of it or not. Each of us is finding a way through which we can best express ourselves.

There is no beginning or ending. All is life, and life is all. All the seeds of life have been sown. All that is the universe, as far as my knowledge takes me, always was and always will be. We are all parts of All That Is, with Spirit embedded within our physical bodies. In miniature, we are All That Is and have access to all the powers of All That Is, according to the evolution of our soul—that is the range that we can receive of all the power that exists.

So that we may co-create—add to, shape, build, deflect, improve, beautify, combine, and do much to birth the Fifth World of Peace and Illumination—the Sacred Parents have provided us, the children of the universe, with all the knowledge and talents necessary. Together, we fashion; we create.

If we are of good intent and desire to use our talents to affirm life, then we are responsible. We are tapping some of the latent powers of the soul.

Our true identities are the spirit within. I often say that if we could realize the power within ourselves, and if we would use that power, it would enable us to heal the world of every dysfunction. Those powers are ours by healing self, by attuning ourselves to higher vibrations of energy, by living responsible lives of service, by entwining with the powers of the *naadin di'i'i*, the guides of the Directions. The more we exercise our connection, the more connected we are. The higher we reach out in acts of love and integrity, the higher are the vibrations to which we respond and the more the truth of purpose that is within us can express itself.

Our spiritual identities are expressed through our physical bodies. If we are of good intent we can perform great service, for we stimulate the sacredness within. But remember that what we express now is but a very small fragment of that which we will one day express. This is growth.

Once we become connected to All That Is around and within, we are outside the realm of dysfunctional influences. We embrace our development so that our spirit power can exert its influence in our expression.

There are no shortcuts. We are dealing with evolution, and it has taken millions of years to bring us to where we are today. Look how far we have come. It is because we evolve that we have arrived at a period of increasing spiritual awareness. These things of spirit require acknowledgment and expression for continued growth.

This is a time where we pay tribute to those who have left the roadmap, the ancients of traditional indigenous societies— for me, the ancestors of the Quero Apache Chiricahua Chihinne Tlish Diyan—who were filled with the power of Spirit, and who strove in their own day to uplift and teach humanity of our sacred heritage.

The knowledge of these Holy Ones was suppressed, nearly forgotten. But, because the power of Spirit moved them, that which they accomplished triumphed over all the fear and separation. Though their faces are now but a part of history, their truth and living-life philosophies live on.

I ask you to learn the lesson of that, for the life you live today is the continuation of those same lives they lived. It is the same truth that you seek to express. Do not seek recognition and validation from those who would be your allies, but live because life is stamped with the seal of sacredness and joy.

For that holy and sacred task we need All Our Relations of goodwill, for we recognize no class, nation, race or color, religion, or lack of religion. We are the children of the Directions—children of the universe. We put forth that we see only life, the service, the efforts made to uplift, to help, and to nurture.

That is the great lesson to learn while walking Tutuskya, the Great Wheel of Life: to be inspired beyond our wildest dreams. Recognize that a soul that is filled with passion to contribute consciously and responsibly to a better tomorrow renders service today. That person bestows love and compassion, using all her power to aid wherever she can those who strive to improve the future for All Our Relations.

Yesterday becomes today, and today becomes tomorrow. Our generation becomes the generations to come. This is the truth of the Seven Generations prophecy.

We strive to uplift All Our Relations, seeing hurts healed, separation replaced by intimacy, ignorance lit by knowledge, fear abolished, and spiritualism grounded. We are the children of the universe. There is no other way for us to be except that we shall evolve into the Fifth World of Peace.

I tell you always the same things. I can only give you in a few simple words the spiritual truths that you have heard many times, in many ways. There is nothing new to add to spiritual truth. All that is necessary is to allow our spiritual natures to function, that we are able to receive more readily the power of Spirit.

guzhuguja juulgu

Exquisitely Ordered

children of Evolution

I pray to Spirit that we may embrace the Sacred Laws of love and compassion that guide the footsteps of evolution. I pray that we may come to a clearer understanding of Spirit and its relationship to all the phenomena of life and to all the children of the universe.

Spirit has been so misunderstood throughout the centuries —misinterpreted, limited, and restricted—that we seek to reveal All That Is as Sacred Law in manifestation. The Sacred Parents are responsible for every manifestation of life; all that exists does so because of their power and their sustenance. The whole order of creation honors this sacred manner of being. The birds, the flowers, the trees, the wind, the ocean, the mountain, the hills and the valleys, the sunshine and the rain, the storm and the lightning—all these are but expressions of the Sacred Parents of all life.

We seek to reveal that all are fashioned in love, that Spirit manifests through our beings, that we move and breathe and live because the Sacred Parents are within us and we are within the Sacred Parents. None has the power to come between the child and the parents, for all the inspiration, all the truth, all the wisdom, all the revelation, all the knowledge that belongs to that infinite reservoir can be reached by each child of the Sacred Parents, as one desires—in aspiration, humility, and service—to become a conduit for that sacred power of evolution.

We seek to reveal the greatness latent within every human soul, the mighty power waiting to be released, pent up through misunderstanding, waiting to surge through the physical being and express spiritual heights in our daily lives. We would seek to make all children live lives in fullness, in beauty, in understanding of the purpose for which we are born, so that we might extract from life all the richness, all the sweetness, all the beauty that is ours for the asking.

We seek to bring the Sacred Parents closer to their children and their children near to them, to overcome all the obstacles that stand in the way, to banish all the restriction and limitations so that the children of this world may know the Sacred Parents and seek to reveal them in service. That is the prayer of this servant, who seeks to serve.

I want you to know that All Your Relations are close to you, even when you cannot hear them, even when it seems that they are invisible, unseen, unheard, unfelt.

All Our Relations are around and about us because they love us, and the love that they have for us makes us always seek to serve All That Is, and, through us, those who require the strength of the Sacred Parents.

The truth that I teach is the truth of potential that knows no bounds and no limitation. It is for all, not just one. It seeks to embrace the whole of humanity within its loving embrace.

May we all become conscious of that mighty power that is around and about us, of the great love that is being poured into our reality, the inspiration that seeks to express itself through us, the truth that is waiting to be revealed, the wisdom that seeks to illumine our evolution. And may we strive through service to the whole to make ourselves accessible to the sacred power of co-creation, so that we may become at one with All Our Relations, so that working in harmony with Sacred Law and filled with wisdom, we may become conduits for All That Is. May the Sacred Parents bless you.

Hiyaa gozhoo dolee. May peace flow.

MARIA YRACÉBŮRŮ

Afterword

I received from my elders a very interesting teaching. Long, long ago, when peoples lived in their individual tribes and groups, they mated and produced children among their own kind. This allowed the passing on from generation to generation of the full and complete knowledge of the parents. Everything—material and spiritual—was naturally passed on and awakened in the individual as it was needed, from one generation to the next. Living in close-knit groups with elders always present, this information and knowledge was brought forward into the individual's life with no effort. It was all there within, simply waiting to be stimulated by the person's lifeway and experience.

Then, peoples began to travel and intermarry. This mixing of bloodlines—among tribes, groups, races—brought about a very interesting result. A new kind of intelligence and creativity was ignited—a sense of individuality and uniqueness, which was part of the evolution of our species. However, as often is the case, there was a trade-off. What was given up was the automatic and natural passage of the lineage of knowledge from generation to generation. Now, it had to be learned from personal internal experience and outer teaching. It had to be consciously passed on and consciously learned.

While people lived in integrated groups, this did not pose such a challenge. Their lives were organized around passing along this vital and powerful lineage. Crafts people, elders, medicine people, spiritual leaders—all people took it upon themselves to share whatever they carried with the younger generation. Time was devoted to learning material skills, and in kivas and medicine lodges, around winter fires, the more esoteric and deep historical knowledge was passed. The people knew that the well-being of the coming generations depended upon the clear and precise passage of this knowledge, as well as the wisdom gained with living it.

In the present time, with the break-up of traditional families, clans, tribes, and other integrated groups, the ritual passage of this vital knowledge has often been almost eliminated. Surface material information is given to children through a very incomplete kind of schooling. Often there are no spiritual teachers present, no winter evenings of passing the ancient wisdom, no attention paid to this important task. And we suffer greatly from this. We are bereft in more ways than we even know, especially about the ways and practices of spirit that uplift our lives, and that, although seeming esoteric, are the baseline of not just living, but living well.

In my own lifetime I have seen (and personally experienced) that the young must have strong intent and persevere with diligence the learning of spiritual ways. Often, even with this intent, it is difficult to find elders who carry the pure lineages, especially among our native peoples. In the case of Native Americans, children of the conquered people were forcibly taken away from their homes and lineages, put in missionary schools, beaten if they spoke their language or practiced any of their spiritual ways. They were indoctrinated from first through twelfth grade— denied their parents, their lifeways, and the passage of ancient knowledge. Only a few children escaped this capture and indoctrination, and they were ones kept in the backcountry, never to be seen by white people. They were very rare.

Even if there were elders available, children often lived separate from them, were busy with schooling, and had little of the day-to-day contact so usual in the past. Thus, the struggle to gain the knowledge of wisdom of the ancient lineages was a great one. This is one of the reasons that what Maria has received from her grandfather Ten Bears and her Quero Apache culture is so rich and so valuable. It is rare and beautiful, and she has devoted her life to its development and sharing.

Another challenge of our time is the attempt to pass knowledge and wisdom through the written word—an essentially mind-oriented practice, when much of the vital wisdom of Spirit is of the heart. The mystical poetry that flows from Maria and the lineage she carries is the finest way we can experience and learn these vital ways. For you to be with her words, commit to the practices, live with this material will serve you well in the development of your spirit, your energetic understandings, your own precious life and lifeway.

We live in a shattered and chaotic time, a time with the clear possibility of the destruction of the human race, or, paradoxically, our upliftment into a golden time of heart and light. Thus it is essential that we find the Path with the Heart. The one we call Dawn Star, the great teacher of the Piscean Age, came to teach us the way of the heart and the magic of Love. White Buffalo Calf Pipe Woman, bringer of the *chanupa,* the sacred pipe, gave us the holy teachings of oneness, unity, and wholeness. We must learn these things if we are to move onward and upward as a human family. The teachings Maria shares are based in this understanding of Love, connection, unity, respect, honoring, and good relationship with All Our Relations. I commend them to you, not as something superfluous but as fundamental and vital to the development we must each make—starting with the silence within and the connection there with our Source and Creator, moving out through our hands and hearts into joyful service to all of Life.

We are the rainbow generation given this tremendous

task. We are meant for it, born to it, given the deep ability to uplift ourselves to a new and beautiful way of being within the Circle of Life. We must be about it, with clear intent and focused diligence, in service not only of ourselves and our families, but of seven generations of All Our Relations.

I HAVE SPOKEN,
BROOKE MEDICINE EAGLE
AUTHOR OF *BUFFALO WOMAN COMES SINGING*